Research on Language and Social Interaction

VOLUME 34, NUMBER 1 — 2001

Table of Contents

Most Commonly Used Transcription Symbols

.	(period) Falling intonation.
?	(question mark) Rising intonation.
,	(comma) Continuing intonation.
-	(hyphen) Marks an abrupt cut-off.
::	(colon(s)) Prolonging of sound.
<u>never</u>	(underlining) Stressed syllable or word.
WORD	(all caps) Loud speech.
°word°	(degree symbols) Quiet speech.
>word<	(more than & less than) Quicker speech.
<word>	(less than & more than) Slowed speech.
hh	(series of h's) Aspiration or laughter.
.hh	(h's preceded by dot) Inhalation.
[ ]	(brackets) Simultaneous or overlapping speech.
=	(equals sign) Contiguous utterances.
(2.4)	(number in parentheses) Length of a silence.
(.)	(period in parentheses) Micro-pause, 2/10 second or less.
( )	(empty parentheses) Non-transcribable segment of talk.
(word)	(word or phrase in parentheses) Transcriptionist doubt.
((gazing toward the ceiling))	(double parentheses) Description of non-speech activity.

Research on Language and Social Interaction, 34(1), 1–13
Copyright © 2001, Lawrence Erlbaum Associates, Inc.

Children's Gender Indexing in Language: From the Separate Worlds Hypothesis to Considerations of Culture, Context, and Power

Amy Kyratzis
Graduate School of Education
University of California, Santa Barbara

In the early 1980s, an influential theory that guided much of the recent work on children's communicative competence, the separate worlds hypothesis (SWH; Maltz & Borker, 1982) gained prominence. The hypothesis states that as a result of separated peer play in childhood, with girls playing predominantly with other girls and boys playing predominantly with other boys, the genders evolve quite different goals for social interactions and communicative styles.

Although a great deal of research with White middle-class children supported the SWH, several critiques were leveled against it by feminist researchers (Bing & Bergvall, 1996; Cameron, 1996; Freed, 1996). These critiques claimed that the theory overdichotomized and universalized gender differences, paying little attention to contextual variation in gender display and neglecting considerations of power in children's and adults' use of gender-linked forms. The first section of this introduction articulates the origin of the SWH and the research that supported it. The second section spells out the feminist critiques. Because the feminist critiques were theoretical and

I am indebted to Susan Ervin-Tripp, Marjorie Goodwin, Amy Sheldon, and Karen Tracy for comments.

Correspondence concerning this article should be sent to Amy Kyratzis, Graduate School of Education, University of California, Santa Barbara, CA 93106. E-mail: Kyratzis@education. ucsb.edu political in nature and based on a only a small number of empirical studies, the research presented in this special issue strengthens the empirical base. The third section articulates how the studies presented in this issue address the shortcomings in past research identified in feminist critiques.

EXPLANATION OF THE SEPARATE WORLDS HYPOTHESIS

The SWH draws on Whiting and Edwards's (1988) systematic observation of early and middle childhood in six cultures, which was based on carefully constructed naturalistic time samples. They found that children tend to segregate in same-sex groups. According to Whiting and Edwards, "the emergence of same-sex preferences in childhood is a cross-cultural universal and robust phenomenon" (p. 81). SWH also was based on observations that the types of activities in which girls and boys engage differ substantially. Boys' games were found to be more competitive, active, and aggressive, requiring larger groups and a more complex social structure. Girls' games, in contrast, were portrayed as more cooperative, passive, and verbal as well as lacking in complex social structure (Lever, 1976).

Using this research, Maltz and Borker (1982) argued that separation in childhood and these vastly different activities in which girls and boys engage lead them to develop different genres of speech and different skills for doing things with words. Extrapolating from Gumperz's (1982) model of interethnic communication, they argued that distinct subcultures evolve in girls' and boys' friendship groups. Girls learn that talk is for (a) creating and maintaining relationships of closeness and equality, (b) criticizing others in acceptable ways, and (c) interpreting accurately the speech of other girls. Boys learn that talk is for (a) asserting a position of dominance, (b) attracting and maintaining an audience, and (c) asserting themselves when another speaker has the floor. Girls' talk is collaboration oriented, and boys' talk is competition oriented. Maltz and Borker (1982), and later Tannen (1990b), proposed that the ways of speaking that adults learn growing up in separate social worlds of peers are so different that male–female communication in our society constitutes "cross-cultural communication" (p. 18), often leading to miscommunication. Maltz and Borker (1982) argued that aspects of behavior are most strongly gender-

differentiated during childhood and that "adult patterns of friendly interaction involve learning to overcome . . . some of the gender-specific cultural patterns typical of childhood" (p. 215).

Maltz and Borker (1982) relied heavily on Goodwin's (1980) data for
their claims. Goodwin reported that the girls in the African American
Philadelphia neighborhood where she observed friendship groups of 9- to
13-year-olds talked negatively about the use of direct commands to equals,
seeing it only as appropriate in speech of older to younger children.
Although disputes were common, girls phrased their arguments and directives in terms of proposals for future action (e.g., "let's . . ."). These mitigated the imposition of the request and helped constitute more egalitarian
social organization.

Since Maltz and Borker's (1982) model was published, several studies have indicated sociolinguistic differences between girls and boys (see
Coates, 1986, for an earlier review). Tannen (1990a) analyzed the conversations of same-sex pairs of best friends, between 8 and 16 years, who
were asked to talk about something serious or intimate. Pairs of male
friends seemed uncomfortable with the task, avoided eye contact, and sat
parallel to one another rather than face to face. Pairs of female friends, in
contrast, seemed more comfortable discussing intimate topics and, when
they did so, supported one another.

Several studies with younger children in the United States, 5 years old
and younger, show differences between girls' and boys' communicative
styles. Miller, Danaher, and Forbes (1986) found that in arguments, 5- to
7-year-old boys used a more heavy-handed style, whereas girls used mitigated strategies, including compromise and evasion. Sheldon (1990),
observing topically similar disputes within a girls' and a boys' triadic
grouping, found that the boys used a more adversarial style than did the
girls. Boys' conflicts were extended and disrupted fantasy play, whereas
girls' conflicts were more likely to be resolved. Girls seemed to strive to
maintain interconnectedness through compromise and conflict resolution.
A study by Kyratzis and Ervin-Tripp (1999) similarly found that among
dyads of 4- and 7-year-old best friends, girls were more likely to sustain a
joint pretense narrative, whereas boys were more likely to lapse into arguments about how to proceed, disrupting joint fantasy. Leaper (1991)
observed 5- and 7-year-olds and found that verbal exchanges among girls
employed collaborative speech acts involving positive reciprocity, whereas exchanges among boys employed speech acts promoting negative reciprocity. Sachs (1987), observing pretend play among groups of preschool

girls and boys, found that girls used more mitigated forms of directives, forms that invited agreement (e.g., "pretend," "let's"), whereas boys used more direct forms of requests (e.g., direct commands and declarative directives—"you have to").

These studies contributed to the view that became established that girls and boys have different sociolinguistic subcultures. In same-sex groups, girls interact to sustain interaction and realize group goals, and boys interact to top or one-up conversational partners and realize self-goals.

FEMINIST CRITIQUES OF SEPARATE WORLDS (AND BROADER THEORIES OF GENDER AND LANGUAGE)

Despite these supportive findings, several critiques have been leveled at the SWH. Some of these critiques apply to views of gender and language more broadly (see Bing & Bergvall, 1996; Freed, 1996); others are unique to the SWH (Cameron, 1996, deals with the latter). Criticism of the SWH and related models of gender and language can be arranged into four main arguments. The first critique is that studies emphasize differences and, in so doing, minimize the extensive overlap and similarities that exist in women's and men's speech. In addition, looking for differences in form might overlook similarities in function. For instance, Goodwin and Goodwin (1987) reported that

> Though there are some differences in the ways in which girls and boys organize their arguing . . . the features they use in common are far more pervasive. Were we to focus only on points where girls and boys differ, the activity itself would be obscured. (p. 205)

Regarding the field's tendency to minimize similarities between women's and men's speech, Sheldon (1996) noted that our views of conflict are androcentric and fail to acknowledge girls' self-assertion. She documented girls using a highly assertive conflict style, *double-voice discourse,* that has an overlay of mitigation and has the effect of softening discord (Sheldon, 1992, 1996).

More recent researchers have found the extent of segregation between girls and boys not to be as great as Whiting and Edwards's (1988) and other characterizations would lead one to believe. Thorne (1993), examining gender segregation in various middle school classrooms in the United

States, reported contextual variation in the degree of gender segregation; factors such as class size, age, and ethnic makeup of the group—and whether classrooms or neighborhoods were observed—affect gender segregation. If girls and boys interact together and are not segregated all of the time, then the assumption of separate subcultures of communication becomes problematic.

A second critique of SWH is that they are essentialist (i.e., treat speech features as invariant, context-free—in the strongest sense—biologically determined qualities of girls and boys) and do not give sufficient emphasis to the role of social practices, activities, and contextual factors in affecting language. A recent special journal issue (Holmes, 1999) entitled "Communities of Practice in Language and Gender Research" embodies this criticism. As Eckert and McConnell-Ginet (1992) claimed, language only indirectly indexes gender: "The relationship is mediated by the social activities and practices—i.e., the communities of practice—in which individuals participate" (Ehrlich, 1999, p. 240).

In terms of the impact of contextual factors, Goodwin (1990) found that girls shifted their style toward using more direct forms of requests when playing with boys rather than with other girls. Goodwin (1993) also found that the form of social organization that evolved in girls' pretend play (playing house) differed from that which characterized their task activities. As she argued, "The fact that girls' social organization varies substantially across different domains makes it imperative that studies of girls' play be grounded in detailed analyses of specific contexts of use" (p. 161). DeHart (1996) found that gender differences found in peer talk (e.g., Sachs, 1987) did not generalize to the sibling context. Thus, it seems important to acknowledge that both girls and boys have a repertoire of speech strategies available to them and that they manipulate speech style for given interactive goals. As Ervin-Tripp (1978) advised:

> Some social settings may emphasize gender and others do not . . . As the reference group shifts, we can expect that individual speakers may "monitor male" or masculinize speech, or "monitor female" or feminize speech . . . What I am proposing here is the examination of situational effects upon styles within the individual's repertoire (p. 24).

A third critique of these dichotomous models of gender and language is that factors such as race, social class, and culture have been largely overlooked (Bing & Bergvall, 1996; Freed, 1996; Goodwin, 1990, 1995, 1998; Ochs, 1992, 1993). In other words, many views of gender and language, including the SWH, are universalist. Assumptions about girls' affiliativeness and niceness, and boys' adversarialness, are based primarily on studying American White middle-class children. These findings have been found to be invalid for African American and Latino communities in the United States (Goodwin, 1990, 1995, 1998) and Chinese communities in Taiwan (Farris, 1991, 2000, in press) and Mainland China (Kyratzis & Guo, 1996).

Some recent research by Ochs (1993) provides a useful framework within which to evaluate cultural variation in gender display. Ochs argued that the relation of language to gender is not a straightforward mapping of linguistic form onto the social meaning of gender; rather, it is constituted and mediated at least partly by the relations of language to "stances" or general interaction poses having to do with how one presents oneself to others (e.g., hesitation or aggression, coarse or delicate intensity) as well as the different valuings of these stances for women and men across different societies. As Ochs noted,

> A more complex representation of language and gender would specify which types of conversational acts, speech activities, affective and epistemological stances, participant roles in situations, and more, enter into the constitution or construction of gender within a particular community and across different communities. (pp. 153–154)

Ochs highlighted the constitutive impact of language on the image of women in different societies. For example, "that WMC American mothers use a simplified register pervasively has a constitutive impact on the image of women in that this practice socializes young children into an image of women as accommodating or addressee-centered in demeanor" (p. 161). In contrast, the practice in Western Samoan households of mothers rarely simplifying speech to children "socializes young children to be accommodating" (p. 161).

A fourth criticism is that these views of gender skirt around problems of power and dominance (Cameron, 1996; Eckert & McConnell-Ginet, 1992; Freed, 1992). Although these studies attribute differences in speech to gender, the difference might be due to power (Ervin-Tripp, 1978). O'Barr and Atkins (1980), for instance, found that the speech behaviors that are often linked to gender (e.g., directness of control moves) reflect one's ranking or power in a given situation, independent of gender.

Cameron (1996) claimed that the relativistic claims of the SWH are comfortable for linguists, who do not want to be evaluative of difference, but relativism nonetheless is problematic:

Different discourse strategies arise in distinct social contexts, and they are used to accomplish different tasks, rather than simply to do the same task in a different way . . . The behavioral differences associated with these positions cannot convincingly be passed off as neutral, accidental, or arbitrary—nor indeed, as purely linguistic. They are rooted in, and they help to maintain, a larger social and political order, in which women and men are destined not simply to differ from one another . . . but in important respects to *complement* one another, to be ideally what "the opposite sex" is not (e.g., nurturant where he is aggressive, intuitive where he is logical) . . . It should be noted that complementarity does not mean equality. On the contrary, gender relations are predicated on the subordination of one group to another . . . To be sure, it makes little sense to argue about whether "status" is better than "intimacy" or vice versa. Nevertheless, if there is a gender-specialization whereby girls learn to seek intimacy and boys to seek status, that is hardly arbitrary in terms of the larger social structure. It could be characterized as a training of boys for public and girls for private life; or as a training for boys in the exercise of power and for girls in its abdication. (pp. 43–44)

In other words, separate spheres of influence means blocked access to desirable domains of activity. This can be detrimental for girls and women, because the male-associated spheres might be more culturally valued or powerful. It can be detrimental for men and boys as well, whose blocked access to domains like home and family also can be undesirable.

Although the SWH does not deal with issues of dominance, there are dominance implications in data from different subcultures. A number of U.S. studies showed that when women and men interact, men appear to dominate (e.g., Zimmerman & West, 1975). Coates (1986) reviewed the literature on the consequences of sociolinguistic style differences, noting

It can be be argued that their competence in a different style disadvantages women in interaction with men. In mixed conversations, women do more of the interactive work, supporting others' topics, respecting others' turns, facilitating conversational flow through the use of questions. The end-product of all this is that male speakers dominate talk. Nor is this fortuitous. Power relations are reproduced through talk, and it would be naive to deny that there must be some relationship between these gender-differentiated conversational styles and existing power structures. (p. 194)

With respect to the consequences of sociolinguistic style differences for children, Coates (1986) reviewed studies by Kelly, Whyte, and Smail (1984), Spender (1982), Sadker and Sadker (1985), and others showing that boys contribute more to classroom discussions and get more attention from teachers. She concluded that boys' and girls' "differentiated communicative competence enables boys to dominate in the classroom. The classroom, in other words, mirrors the outside world: male dominance is acted out in the classroom, and this limits girls' opportunities to learn" (p. 196). However, as noted by Coates, Swann (1988) pointed out that the idea of males dominating classroom talk risks oversimplifying things. Swann found that there was contextual variation in the dominance strategies, suggesting that these differences were not categorical. Moreover, she found that girls and teachers colluded in boys' dominance and that "it is likely that everyone is an accomplice in the tendency by boys to contribute more to classroom talk" (p. 139).

Extending this notion of girls and boys colluding in the expression of male dominance, researchers have begun to attend to speakers' deliberate monitoring of gender display, emphasizing that speakers can strategically manipulate stylistic features of language. Lakoff (1975) first raised this possibility in her book, referring to it as "bilingualism." The problem, she noted, was not in women's ability to style shift but in the ramifications of doing so. Freed (1992) noted that, in certain contexts such as courtship rituals, males adjust to speak more sensitively. In girls' and boys' groups in a preschool in Beijing, Farris (1991) suggested that children collectively monitor one another for gender display. In addition, in cross-sex talk girls use more direct commands than they did in speech with other girls (Goodwin, 1980). The question then becomes, why girls sometimes choose assertive forms and other times do not.

To summarize, the SWH provided the field with an excellent starting point for thinking about how children construct gender. This viewpoint gave children an active, constructive role in the production of gendered styles of behavior and research with U.S. middle-class children has substantiated many of its claims. However, feminist critiques have raised several problems with the separate cultures view of girls' and boys' speaking styles, particularly issues of universalism, essentialism, and failure to consider how power interacts with gender. Although the feminist critiques have been persuasive, they have been based on a small number of empirical studies and have been primarily theoretical in thrust. More empirical research with children is needed to test the claims.

CHILDREN'S GENDER INDEXING: CONSIDERATIONS OF CULTURE, CONTEXT, AND POWER

The studies in this special issue remedy this omission and build on the view of gender as "an achieved property of situated conduct . . . carried out in the presence of others who are presumed to be oriented to its production" (West & Zimmerman, 1987, p. 126). The articles show the importance of culture, context, and power for children's gender construction. In particular, the studies focus on the language of middle-class Japanese and Chinese children, middle-class American children of multiple ethnicities, and working-class Latino children. In terms of contextual variation, activity settings such as home, classroom, and recess time in school are studied. As pointed out earlier, the power implications of separate communicative subcultures for girls and boys have been thought to be particularly important for cross-sex talk in the school setting. Activity settings also might affect girls' and boys' language in cross-sex talk in that the relative expertise of girls and boys in given activity domains might be asymmetrical.

Expertise might determine whether assertive forms are used and whether girls or boys use more assertive forms in cross-sex talk. Studying the same children, at different levels of expertise, allows examination of the influences of expertise independent of gender. Different domains can be instantiated in children's pretend play. Similarly, observing cross-sex talk among children when different themes or frames are instantiated would allow assessing whether power allocation is gender linked by domain. The articles in this issue examine these possible ways in which the speech features we associate with gender might be linked to power and interact with culture and activity type.

ISSUE PREVIEW

The first two articles are about preschool children's language. Keiko Nakamura's article examines preschoolers' socialization into Japanese, a language in which gender marking is inescapable. Documenting many of the rich ways in which gender indexing can be accomplished in Japanese, Nakamura provides support for girls' cooperative language and boys' competitive language. Although her findings are partly consistent with the SWH, Nakamura's study documents strong contextual variation in children's gender indexing.

The article by Amy Kyratzis and Jiansheng Guo compares Mandarin-speaking preschoolers' language in Mainland China with that of English-speaking preschoolers in the United States. With a focus on conflict strategies, the article provides no support for girls' cooperative language as a cultural universal. Although U.S. preschool girls used rather indirect conflict strategies, in Mainland China, girls' conflict strategies were very direct. In addition, the analysis revealed that in cross-sex conflict girls in both cultures dominated in some contexts but not in others. There is contextual complexity in the conflict strategies that are learned and expressed in same-sex groups. The analysis suggests that one source of this complexity might derive from the fact that girls and boys collude in allocating power in gender-linked ways.

The next two articles deal with middle-school-age children. The article by Marjorie Harness Goodwin deals with the influence of expertise. The analysis examines how expertise affects the directness of children's request forms. Based on a longitudinal study of talk within a mixed-sex friendship group of fourth- to sixth-grade children during recess, the study enables examination of the influence of changing levels of expertise on the talk. At the beginning, the girls in the group had greater expertise in jump rope. However, at a later point, the girls and boys had equivalent expertise. Goodwin's analysis documents that expertise (and hence, power), rather than gender, determines the directness of the request forms.

The article by Jenny Cook-Gumperz and Margaret Szymanski examines talk within a mixed-sex group of Latino children doing groupwork. The teacher frames the groupwork as interaction within a domestic or family frame. In this study, Cook-Gumperz and Szymanski explore the interaction of culture, context, and power. Within Latino culture, the authors argue, this frame licenses girls to be powerful. Girls use assertive strategies during groupwork. For the girls, the role of female cooperative peer group member interfaces with the family role of a big sister. The teacher's framing of the interaction renders the family frame relevant in the school context—hence harnessing Latina power and assertiveness in cross-sex classroom talk.

The issue concludes with an epilogue by Susan Ervin-Tripp in which she comments on the articles and critically examines the problem of gender indexing. Ervin-Tripp questions whether children use the features we associate with gender to index femininity and masculinity, and considers how the use of these stylistic features interact with activity context, culture, and power. In addition, she argues for the importance of considering the social networks in which children participate, identifying the influence of children's membership and placement within different kinds of peer (e.g., home and school), family, and friendship groups on their speech styles. Ervin-Tripp gives an especially rich picture of the complex ways in which these factors interact to influence use of the speech features we associate with gender, including (a) friendship networks exert pressure to participate in particular types of activities, (b) the composition of groups appears to affect speech in large measure through the choice of activity, and (c) activity settings exert their influence through intervening factors such as power and territory (which in turn depend on norms developed within the social network, age, and cultural context).

This special issue, then, examines gender construction by children in some of its rich cultural and contextual complexity as well as in some of its interactions with power.

REFERENCES

Bing, J. M., & Bergvall, V. L. (1996). The question of questions: Beyond binary thinking. In V. L. Bergvall, J. M. Bing, & A. F. Freed (Eds.), *Rethinking language and gender research: Theory and practice* (pp. 1–30). London: Longman.

Cameron, D. (1996). The language–gender interface: Challenging co-optation. In V. L. Bergvall, J. M. Bing, & A. F. Freed (Eds.), *Rethinking language and gender research: Theory and practice* (pp. 31–53). London: Longman.

Coates, J. (1986). *Women, men, and language* (2nd ed.). London: Longman.

DeHart, G. B. (1996). Gender and mitigation in 4-year-olds' pretend play talk with siblings. *Research on Language and Social Interaction, 29,* 81–96.

Eckert, P., & McConnell-Ginet, S. (1992). Think practically and look locally: Language and gender as community-based practice. *Annual Review of Anthropology, 21,* 461–490.

Ehrlich, S. (1999). Communities of practice, gender, and the representation of sexual assault. *Language in Society, 28,* 239–256.

Ervin-Tripp, S. M. (1978). 'What do women sociolinguists want?' Prospects for a research field. *International Journal of the Sociology of Language, 17,* 17–28.

Farris, C. S. (1991). The gender of child discourse: Same-sex peer socialization through language use in a Taiwanese preschool. *Journal of Linguistic Anthropology, 2,* 198–224.

Farris, C. S. (2000). Cross-sex peer conflict and the discursive production of gender in a Chinese preschool in Taiwan. *Journal of Pragmatics, 32,* 539–568.

Farris, C. S. (in press). Silence and speaking: Preschool students in Taiwan discursively produce Chinese gendered subjectivities. *Anthropology and Education Quarterly.*

Freed, A. (1992). We understand perfectly: A critique of Tannen's view of cross-sex communication. In K. Hall, M. Bucholtz, & B. Moonwomon (Eds.), *Locating power:*

Proceedings of the second Berkeley women and language conference (pp. 144–152). Berkeley, CA: Berkeley Women and Language Group.

Freed, A. (1996). Language and gender research in an experimental setting. In V. L. Bergvall, J. M. Bing, & A. F. Freed (Eds.), *Rethinking language and gender research: Theory and practice* (pp. 54–76). London: Longman.

Goodwin, M. H. (1980). Directive/response speech sequences in girls' and boys' talk activities. In S. McConnell-Ginet, R. Borker, & N. Furman (Eds.), *Women and language in literature and society* (pp. 157–173). New York: Praeger.

Goodwin, M. H. (1990). *He-said-she-said: Talk as social organization among black children.* Bloomington: Indiana University Press.

Goodwin, M. H. (1993). Accomplishing social organization in girls' play: Patterns of competition and cooperation in an African-American working-class girls' group. In S. T. Hollis, L. Pershing, & M. J. Young (Eds.), *Feminist theory and the study of folklore* (pp. 149–165). Urbana: University of Illinois Press.

Goodwin M. H. (1995). Co-construction in girls' hopscotch. *Research on Language and Social Interaction, 28,* 261–282.

Goodwin, M. H. (1998). Games of stance: Conflict and footing in hopscotch. In S. Hoyle & C. T. Adger (Eds.), *Language practices of older children* (pp. 23–46). New York: Oxford University Press.

Goodwin, M. H., & Goodwin, C. (1987). Children's arguing. In S. U. Phelips, S. Steele, & C. Tanz (Eds.), *Language, gender and sex in comparaative perspective* (pp. 200–248). Cambridge, England: Cambridge University Press.

Gumperz, J. J. (1982). *Language and social identity.* Cambridge, England: Cambridge University Press.

Holmes, J. (Ed.). (1999). Communities of practice in language and gender research [Special issue]. *Language in Society, 28*(2).

Kelly, A., Whyte, J., & Smail, B. (1984). *Girls into science technology: Final report.* Manchester, England: Equal Opportunities Commission.

Kyratzis, A., & Ervin-Tripp, S. M. (1999). The development of discourse markers in peer interaction. *Journal of Pragmatics, 31,* 1321–1338.

Kyratzis, A., & Guo, J. (1996). "Separate worlds" for girls and boys?: Views from U.S. and Chinese mixed-sex friendship groups. In D. I. Slobin, J. Gerhardt, A. Kyratzis, & J. Guo (Eds.), *Social interaction, social context, and language: Essays in honor of Susan Ervin-Tripp* (pp. 555–578). Mahwah, NJ: Lawrence Erlbaum Associates, Inc.

Lakoff, R. (1975). *Language and woman's place.* New York: Harper & Row.

Leaper, C. (1991). Influence and involvement: Age, gender, and partner effects. *Child Development, 62,* 797–811.

Lever, J. R. (1976). Sex differences in the games children play. *Social Problems, 23,* 478–487.

Maltz, D. N., & Borker, R. A. (1982). A cultural approach to male–female miscommunication. In J. J. Gumperz (Ed.), *Communication, language and social identity* (pp. 196–216). Cambridge, England: Cambridge University Press.

Miller, P., Danaher, D., & Forbes, D. (1986). Sex-related strategies for coping with interpersonal conflict in children aged five and seven. *Developmental Psychology, 22,* 543–548.

O'Barr, W., & Atkins, S. (1980). "Women's language" or "powerless language"? In S. McConnell-Ginet, R. Borker, & N. Furman (Eds.), *Women and language in literature and society* (pp. 93–110). New York: Praeger.

Ochs, E. (1992). Indexing gender. In A. Duranti & C. Goodwin (Eds.), *Rethinking context: Language as an interactive phenomenon. Studies in the social and cultural foundations of language* (Vol. 11, pp. 335–358). Cambridge, England: Cambridge University Press.

Ochs, E. (1993). Indexing gender. In B. D. Miller (Ed.), *Sex and gender hierarchies* (pp. 146–169). Cambridge, England: Cambridge University Press.

Sachs, J. (1987). Preschool girls' and boys' language use in pretend play. In S. U. Phillips, S. Steele, & C. Tanz (Eds.), *Language, gender, and sex in comparative perspective* (pp. 178–188). Cambridge, England: Cambridge University Press.

Sadker, M., & Sadker, D. (1985, March). Sexism in the schoolroom of the '80's. *Psychology Today*, 54–57.

Sheldon, A. (1990). Pickle fights: Gendered talk in preschool disputes. *Discourse Processes, 13*, 5–31.

Sheldon, A. (1992). Conflict talk: Sociolinguistic challenges to self-assertion and how young girls meet them. *Merrill-Palmer Quarterly, 38*, 95–117.

Sheldon, A. (1996). You can be the baby brother but you aren't born yet: Preschool girls' negotiation for power and access in pretend play. *Research on Language and Social Interaction, 29*, 57–80.

Spender, D. (1982). *Invisible women—the schooling scandal.* London: Writers and Readers Publishing Cooperative.

Swann, J. (1988). Talk control: An illustration from the classroom of problems in analysing male dominance in education. In J. Coates & D. Cameron (Eds.), *Women in their speech communities* (pp. 122–140). London: Longman.

Tannen, D. (1990a). Gender differences in topical coherence: Physical alignment and topical cohesion. In B. Dorval (Ed.), *Conversational organization and its development* (pp. 167–206). Norwood, NJ: Ablex.

Tannen, D. (1990b). *You just don't understand: Women and men in conversation.* New York: Ballantine Books.

Thorne, B. (1993). *Gender play: Girls and boys in school.* New Brunswick, NJ: Rutgers University Press.

West, C., & Zimmerman, D. H. (1987). Doing gender. *Gender & Society, 1*, 125–151.

Whiting, B. B., & Edwards, C. (1988). *Children of different worlds.* Cambridge, MA: Harvard University Press.

Zimmerman, D., & West, C. (1975). Sex roles, interruptions, and silences in conversations. In B. Thorne & N. Henley (Eds.), *Language and sex: Difference and dominance* (pp. 105–129). Rowley, MA: Newbury House.

Research on Language and Social Interaction, 34(1), 15–43

Gender and Language in Japanese Preschool Children

Keiko Nakamura
Institute of Cultural and Linguistic Studies
Keio University

This article explores the relation between gender and language use in Japanese preschool children. Gender-based differences in Japanese include phonological, lexical, and morphosyntactical differences, as well as differences in conversational style (e.g., Shibamoto, 1985).

The data come from monthly naturalistic observations of 24 monolingual Japanese boys and girls (ages 3–6) engaged in same-sex peer play. The results show that appropriate usage of gender-based linguistic distinctions emerges quite early (e.g., use of different sentence-final particles, addressee–reference terms, lexical forms). In addition, as early as age 3, most children preferred to play with same-sex friends and had distinct preferences in their play activities. Analyses of boys' and girls' speech used during same-sex peer interactions show differences in communicative style and use of specific linguistic forms. Furthermore, language use was related closely to the nature of the play context.

According to the separate worlds hypothesis in gender research, boys and girls spend much of their time in the preschool and elementary school

This study was funded by a Fulbright Graduate Research Award from the U.S.–Japan Educational Commission, a Woodrow Wilson Women's Studies Grant for Doctoral Candidates, a Doctoral Dissertation Improvement Grant from the National Science Foundation, a Minority Fellowship Program Dissertation Support Grant from the American Psychological Association, an Affirmative Action Dissertation-Year Fellowship from the University of California, and a Dissertation Fellowship from the Spencer Foundation.

Correspondence concerning this article should be sent to Keiko Nakamura, Institute of Cultural and Linguistic Studies, Keio University, 4-14-18-5 Himonya, Meguro-ku, Tokyo 152-0003, Japan. E-mail: kei@aya.yale.edu years in same-sex friendship groups, boys playing mainly with other boys and girls playing mainly with other girls (Maccoby, 1990; Maltz & Borker, 1982). Consequently, girls and boys evolve very different "cultures," involving different interaction styles and goals for interactive exchanges (Tannen, 1990). As described in the introduction to this issue, girls' speech has been described as collaborative or affiliative, based on solidarity and support (e.g., making suggestions, avoiding conflict, and competition). On the other hand, boys' speech has been described as adversarial, control oriented, and competitive (e.g., giving orders, disagreeing, engaging in conflict; Goodwin, 1980; Kyratzis & Guo, 1996; Sheldon, 1990; Tannen, 1990). Overall, such accounts describe boys' interactive style as focusing on self, whereas girls' interactive style seems to be more concerned with group goals.[1] As researchers such as Whiting and Edwards (1988) claim that "the emergence of same-sex preferences in childhood is a cross-culturally universal and robust phenomenon" (p. 81), consequently one might wonder whether gender differences in language and interactive style are universal across cultures.

Gender roles are defined more clearly in Japanese society than in Western countries. It has been found that countries with large wage discrepancies between men and women (i.e., Japan, as opposed to countries such as Denmark and the United States) have lower levels of male participation in household chores (as reported in Shimizu et al., 1996, p. 100). An international survey conducted by the Tokyo Metropolitan Government in 1993 showed stronger beliefs in the division of labor in Japan as compared to other countries (cited in Bandoo, 1998). For example, "doing laundry" was reported to be the wife's responsibility according to 91.3% of 1,560 Japanese adult respondents, as opposed to 74.6% of 611 U.S. respondents and 80.8% of 781 Swedish respondents. Similarly, "preparing meals" was the wife's responsibility according to 91.5% of the Japanese respondents and 71.0% of the U.S. respondents. According to another survey on the equality of men and women administered by the Prime Minister's Office in 1992, a majority of both male (65.7% of 1,553 adults) and female (55.5% of 1,971 adults) respondents believed that "men should work outside the home, and women should work in the home (e.g., child-rearing, housework)" (cited in Shimizu et al., 1996, p. 101). Although beliefs about division of labor have been weakening since the 1970s, the burdens of childrearing and housework still tend to fall heavily on women. Therefore, many Japanese women choose to quit their jobs on getting married or having children and reenter the workforce after their children start elementary school or kindergarten (Yamamoto, 1997).

As in many Western cultures, in Japan, considerable gender social-ization takes place before children even enter preschool (e.g., Block, 1983; Rheingold & Cook, 1975).[2] Japanese adults usually have different expectations of boys and girls and treat them quite differently. As one might expect, baby girls are dressed differently from baby boys. Boys are given blocks, trucks, and superhero figures, whereas girls are provided with stuffed animals, dolls, and kitchen sets. A rambunctious boy is viewed in a positive manner, as "healthy" or "energetic," whereas a ram-bunctious girl is viewed negatively, as "tomboyish" or "loud." Mothers of boys often hope that their boys develop cheerful and robust personalities, with lots of *genki* 'health, vigor, cheerfulness,' whereas mothers of girls rarely use such qualities as desirable traits for their girls (Peak, 1991). Gender socialization also comes from nonparental sources, such as the media. For example, Japanese children's books and television program-ming are reported to be highly gender stereotyped (e.g., Inoue & Ehara, 1995; Sato, 1977).

In addition, Japanese preschool educators often say that they treat boys and girls equally, but reports of preschool life frequently show dif-ferential treatment according to sex. For example, ethnographic re-searchers have reported that boys are allowed to fight in the classroom, whereas girls are encouraged to intervene and attend to the needs of younger children (e.g., Tobin, Wu, & Davidson, 1989). Researchers such as Imamura (1993) criticize Japanese schools for having an unofficial cur-riculum that enforces gender role behavior (Imamura, 1993). As in the case of children in Western cultures, Japanese preschool children usually prefer to play in same-sex peer groups by age 4 (Maccoby, 1988; Paley, 1984; Peak, 1991). Girls often prefer activities such as playing house, tea party, and traditional singing games, whereas boys enjoy rough-and-tum-ble play, playing with trucks, and playing superheroes.

One crucial aspect of gender socialization in young Japanese children is the acquisition of gender-appropriate language. Knowledge of gender-appropriate language is crucial for speakers of Japanese to communicate effectively in Japanese society. Gender-based differences in Japanese include phonological, lexical, and morphosyntactical differences, as well as differences in conversational style (e.g., Shibamoto, 1985). However, at this point, it is also important to note that one of the myths of the Japanese language is that there are many linguistic features used exclusively by one sex. These days, most Japanese tend to use a variety of styles, according to the conversational context. For example, there are occasions when men use a softer, more empathetic "feminine" style (e.g., when talking to babies) and times when women use a more blunt, "masculine" style (e.g., at work).

Previous studies on Japanese language acquisition have shown that even young children (age 3 and older) are able to make gender-based linguistic distinctions (e.g., Ide, 1979; Nakamura, 1997a, 1997b; Okubo, 1967; Sakata, 1990; Takahashi, 1969). For example, they are able to use appropriate addressee–reference terms in casual speech, such as *boku* and *ore* for male first-person reference, *atashi* for female first-person reference, and *omae* and *kimi* for second-person reference (when boys refer to social equals or inferiors). Furthermore, they use gender-appropriate sentence-final particles such as *wa* (female), *kashira* (female), *zo* (male), and *ze* (male).[3] Boys also quickly adopt male lexical forms such as *dekkai* 'big' (male) and tend to show an early tendency to use Sino-Japanese compound words (e.g., *fukuzatsu* 'complicated,' *henshin* 'transformation').[4] Phonological differences, such as the use of nonstandard pronunciation in the form of phonological reductions by boys (e.g., *tabenee* for the standard *tabenai* 'won't eat') and differences in pitch and intonation also appear by age 3. In general, girls tend to use gender-neutral forms during everyday speech contexts, but during role play, they are able to use "feminine" linguistic markers and conversational style. It is clear that in the case of Japanese, gender is an integral part of language socialization, the process by which children learn to use language in a culture-appropriate manner.

As most Japanese children spend the first few years of their lives in close contact with women (i.e., mothers, day care teachers, preschool teachers), same-sex peer play serves a crucial role as an agent for gender and language socialization, particularly for boys. It has been observed that Japanese boys use more masculine forms during same-sex peer play than during mother–child play contexts, in which they tend to use gender-neutral forms (Nakamura, 1997a, 1997b). During both same-sex peer play and mother–child play, girls tend to use gender-neutral forms, with some "feminine" forms. As most previous research has focused on mother–child interactions, this study examines gender differences in language use during same-sex peer play.

In addition, it has been found that young Japanese children vary their usage of gender-based linguistic differences depending on the nature of the interactional context (Nakamura, 1997b). For example, when boys engage in rough-and-tumble play, they use a large proportion of "masculine" linguistic forms, but when they engage in object construction, their language is more gender neutral. Therefore, it is not surprising that when boys' and girls' language use are compared within a specific interactional context (e.g., a specific play activity requiring specific types of interactional moves), differences in usage of gender-based linguistic forms are reduced. This is discussed later, as the following examples are taken from different types of play scenarios (e.g., superhero pretend play, store play, kitchen play), involving a variety of interactional moves in which children use a wide range of gender-based linguistic distinctions.

METHOD

The data come from a larger project examining sociolinguistic development in Japanese preschool children in which monthly naturalistic observations of 12 boys and 12 girls (ages 3–6) were audiotaped and videotaped (Nakamura, 1997b). The children are from middle-class Japanese families living in the Tokyo metropolitan area. The project was longitudinal, and the data were collected over the course of 1 to 3 years. The children were observed as they played with a variety of interactants (i.e., mothers, siblings, peers, unfamiliar adults). During the peer play sessions, the children were asked to choose a favorite friend to play with (the same friend was used for all of the monthly sessions) and were allowed to engage in play activities of their choice (e.g., pretend play, rough-and-tumble play, object construction), either by choosing from toy props provided by the experimenter or by selecting their own toys. All of the children in the study were attending some form of preschool, either *hoikuen* 'day-care programs' or *yoochien* 'kindergartens.'

RESULTS

As early as age 3, most of the children preferred to play with same-sex friends and showed distinct gender-based preferences in their play activities. As found in Western cultures, Japanese boys liked to play with blocks; engage in object construction (e.g., sculpting, drawing); and play with toys such as trains, cars, and puzzles (e.g., Block, 1983).[5] When

TABLE 1
Play Activities of Japanese Boys by Age (% of Total Time)

Activity	3-Year-Olds	4-Year-Olds	5-Year-Olds
Superheroes	29.4	30.0	19.2
Store	5.9	10.0	19.2
Doctor	0.0	3.3	3.8
House	5.9	3.3	3.8
Trains/planes/cars	0.0	10.0	15.4
Puzzles	11.8	10.0	15.4
Art (e.g., drawing)	11.8	10.0	7.7
Blocks	23.5	23.3	15.4
Rough and tumble	11.8	0.0	0.0

TABLE 2
Play Activities of Japanese Girls by Age (% of Total Time)

Activity	3-Year-Olds	4-Year-Olds	5-Year-Olds
House	25.0	25.0	15.9
Store	15.0	18.8	11.4
Doctor	15.0	6.3	6.8
Zoo	5.0	0.0	0.0
School	0.0	6.3	4.5
Princess/Sailor Moon	0.0	0.0	9.1
Trains/planes/cars	5.0	0.0	0.0
Puzzles	5.0	6.3	0.0
Art (e.g., origami)	15.0	25.0	13.6
Blocks	15.0	9.4	20.5
Games/singing	0.0	3.1	15.9
Reading	0.0	0.0	2.3

engaging in pretend play, they often chose to play superheroes or act out store scenarios. Girls, on the other hand, preferred to play house with dolls or stuffed animals and were willing to try many different pretend play scenarios (e.g., store, zoo, doctor, school). The oldest girls liked to pretend to be princesses or Sailor Moon, a popular television "supergirl" who defeats evil monsters. They also enjoyed object construction (e.g., drawing, origami, sculpting), and the oldest 5-year-old girls enjoyed playing games. Girls often were willing to play with many of the toys that boys typically play with (e.g., blocks), but it was difficult to get boys to play with toys associated with girls (e.g., tea sets). This tendency increased with age. Boys sometimes were willing to try girls' toys when playing with their mothers but refused to do so when playing with other boys.

Gender-Based Linguistic Differences in Same-Sex Peer Play

One major difference between boys' and girls' speech differences during same-sex peer play was their use of gender-based language. Although boys used a variety of masculine speech forms during same-sex peer play (e.g., as compared to when they were conversing with their mothers), girls tended to use gender-neutral speech during same-sex peer play, except during pretend play, when assuming the roles of older women. Even 3-year-olds used various gender-based linguistic forms (e.g., use of different sentence-final particles, addressee–reference terms, lexical forms). Analyses of boys' and girls' speech used during same-sex peer interactions showed clear differences in language style. As seen in the dialogues provided, boys used more assertive and adversarial language, such as sentence-final particles such as *zo* (assertion) and *yo* (emphasis), whereas girls often used more collaborative language, such as interactive particles such as *ne* (requesting or giving confirmation) and *no* (requesting or giving explanation).

DIALOGUE 1: Superheroes scene with two boys (Ryota, 4;3, and Masaki, 4;3), with Ryota's younger brother Keita (2;9) watching on side.[6] Ryota is chasing after Masaki, running around room wildly with robot in hand:

1 Ryota: konna no oshiri penpen da yo! oshiri penpen da yo!
pen pen pen!
I'm going to spank you! I'm going to spank you!
Whack, whack, whack!

2 Masaki: YAMETE!
STOP!

3 Ryota: yoshi.
Okay. ((continues to hit Masaki's superhero doll with his robot))

4 Ryota: sutoraiki!
Strike!

5 Keita: sutoraiki!
Strike!

6 Ryota: nan da! mane suru na!
What? Don't copy (me)! ((threatening Keita with robot))

7 Ryota: gattai! itete - itee! chotto matte-kure- gao-tte
kaijuu ni naru ze!
Merge! ((loud scream)) *Ouch - ouch!* ((bangs foot on table, conversation with mother looking at Ryota's

foot)) *Wait a minute-* ((gruff voice))- *(I'll) become*
a monster- "growl"!

8   Masaki: kaijuu da!
It's a monster! ((playing monsters and superheroes,
running around wildly))

9   Ryota: gomennasai <u>boku</u> wa tatakai dekinain desu. aa-to batan!
Sorry, I can't fight (any more). Ugh- flop!

10   Masaki: urusai <u>zo</u> . . . tetora boi <u>ketchaku</u> ne!
Shut up . . . Tetra-boy, let's settle it!
((run around again, banging on each other))

11   Ryota: nee, dairenken ga nai <u>zo</u>!
Hey, the 'super-sword' is missing!

12   Masaki: dairenken-tte <u>sa</u>, kono koto?
The 'super-sword', you mean this?
((holding up a plastic sword))

13   Ryota: aa.
Yeah.
((slight break in interaction))

14   Ryota: urutoraman sebun da! <u>boku</u> wa hontoo no urutoraman
sebun da! shuu! bakaan! Urutoraman Reo!
(I'm) Ultraman Seven! I'm the real Ultraman Seven!
Whoosh! Bang! Ultraman Leo!

15   Masaki: iku <u>zo</u>. Urutoraman Sebun.
Here (I) go Ultraman Seven!
((a new battle scene unfolds))

In this typical superhero scene, Ryota and Masaki take turns playing various superheroes and monsters, running around and hitting each other over and over again.[7] In this dialogue, we can see that both boys are able to use masculine linguistic forms, such as the masculine sentence-final particles *zo* (lines 10, 11, 15) and *ze* (line 7), which are used to mark assertions, in an emphatic manner. They also use unmitigated requests in the form of imperatives, commands, and prohibitions to order each other around (e.g., *mane suru na* 'don't copy me,' line 6; *matte-kure* 'wait for me,' line 7). Furthermore, they use *boku,* the masculine first-person pronoun, to refer to themselves. In addition, the boys use several Sino-Japanese compound words, words that usually are considered too difficult to be used by children, such as *gattai* 'merge' (line 7) and *ketchaku* 'conclusion' (line 10). These words appear frequently in boys' animated cartoons, such as *Poke-*

mon and *Dragonball Z.* Television speech models for boys clearly provide gender-stereotyped input differing from that of girls' programming. The boys also use nonstandard pronunciation, such as *itee* for *itai* 'ouch' (line 7).[8] Throughout the dialogue, the boys use informal *-da* verb endings (e.g., lines 1,6, 8, 14) and only use formal predicate endings when in role (e.g., line 9, when Ryota plays the role of the dying monster).

As seen in this dialogue, during peer play, especially rough-and-tumble pretend play of this sort, boys tend to use masculine linguistic forms frequently. They use these forms often to mark self-assertion and commands, which form the majority of their interactions in this type of context. A look at a typical kitchen scene with two girls illustrates the difference between the two styles of interaction:

DIALOGUE 2: Kitchen scene with two girls (Yukako, 3;9, and Mika, 3;9). Mika has been playing with the kitchen set; Yukako comes over to play.

1 Mika: ja omamagoto setto de ne: ja Yukako-chan kore yatte
mite kureru ka naa? totte- uwaa:!(.) dete-kichatta!
*And with the kitchen set: (I) wonder if you would try
this for me. Take it off- aaa!. (.)it came out!*
((passing some toy food items over to Yukako, Mika
takes apart the toy rice ball, and a piece of fish
comes flying out))

2 Yukako: onigiri no detekichatta- a:a. ano ne(.) <u>atashi</u> ne (.)
onigiri hitori de ne- nikai tsukutta no- hitori de
sorekara jibun de tsukutta no- jibun de tsukutta no-
<u>Mika-chan</u>.
*The rice ball's (fish) came out- uh-oh. You know I
made rice balls by myself twice, by myself- And
then, (I) made them by myself- (I) made them by
myself- Mika.* ((Mika ignores Yukako and goes on
playing with her toy rice ball.))

3 Mika: aa koo yatte dashite ne- koo yatte yaru no. sorede
koo yatte ne, dekita! batazuke tsukutte-ageru
kara . . . batazuke. Batazuke konnaka ni haitteru kara
batazuke motte kuru kara- baibai!
*(You) take them out like this- you know, and (you) do
it like this. And then (you) do it like this, and it's
done! (I'll) make you butter-saute (fish). The butter
saute is in here, so (I'll) bring it- bye-bye!*

4 Yukako: o-nori maku to detekichau <u>yo ne</u>.
           When (you) wrap it with seaweed, it comes out, doesn't
           it?

5 Mika: norimaki ga arimashita.
           (Here's) the norimaki.

6 Yukako: <u>watashi</u> wa <u>o-ringo</u> no kawa muku kara Mika-chan wa
           batayaki tsukutte.
           I'll peel the apple, so you make the butter sauté.

7 Mika: <u>o-ringo</u> wa ne tsukanai no. tsukanain da yo.
           The apple doesn't stick. (It) doesn't stick.
           ((The toy apple is cut to look like a rabbit, but the
           peel (the ears) has fallen off.))

8 Yukako: dooshite?
           Why?

9 Mika: torechatta no.
           It came off.

10 Yukako: nani ga?
           What did?

11 Mika: torechatta no, kawa ga. <u>chotto</u> kashite. hora ne,
           tsukanai <u>deshoo</u>? ja tomato kitte, hoochoo de ne.
           (It) came off, the peel. Lend (that to me) a bit.
           You see, it doesn't stick, right? Okay, then cut this
           tomato with a knife. ((Mika sees that there is only
           one knife and cutting board))

12 Yukako: manaita ga nai, hoochoo ga nai.
           (I) don't have a cutting board, (I) don't have a
           knife. ((Mika quickly brings over a substitute cutting
           board and miniature knife.))

13 Mika: a ja kore demo ii?
           Oh, is this okay?

14 Yukako: ii yo.
           (It's) okay.

15 Mika: demo daijoobu?
           But is (it) alright? ((referring to the small size of
           the knife))

16 Yukako: kireru yo.
           (It) can cut.

Here we see that Mika and Yukako rarely use so-called "feminine" linguistic forms in the interaction. They do not use feminine sentence-final particles such as *wa* and *kashira*, but they do use combinations of particles such as *yo ne* (line 4), which are considered to be feminine. They also use particles such as *ne* (lines 1–4, 11) and *no* (lines 2, 3, 9, 11). Interactive particles such as *ne* (requesting or giving confirmation) and *no* (requesting or giving explanation) help keep the channel open between the interlocutors by asking for (or giving) feedback in the form of opinions or explanations. Mika also uses *deshoo* 'right?' (line 11) to ask for Yukako's feedback. *Deshoo,* used with a rising intonation, asks for the listener's agreement in a soft and indirect manner (Makino & Tsutsui, 1986). The girls also are able to use feminine first-person pronouns such as *atashi* (line 2) and *watashi* (line 6). Instead of using a second-person pronoun, like other girls, they refer to each other by first name plus *chan* (a diminutive), as in Mika-chan (line 2). The girls also use hedges such as *chotto* 'a little' (line 11) and often are hesitant (e.g., when bringing up new topics, as in line 2, *aa ano ne* 'um, you know'). As is common in the speech of many Japanese women, the girls also engage in repetition (lines 2, 3, 7) and postposing of subjects and objects (e.g., line 11, subject postposed, then object postposed; Shibamoto, 1985). Commands are rare, and requests often are mitigated or polite (e.g., *yatte-mite-kurenai ka naa?* 'I wonder if you would try this for me?' in line 1). Finally, they often use beautification honorifics (e.g., nouns with the polite prefix *o-*), as in *o-ringo* 'apple' and *o-nori* 'seaweed,' which often are used by women to make utterances sound more gentle and refined (Shibamoto, 1985).

The girls often ask for permission (line 13) and give permission (line 14), and they ask questions (lines 8, 10, 15) and give answers (lines 9, 11, 16). Their requests are mitigated, and they rarely use direct commands. The girls avoid the appearance of hierarchy and mitigate attempts to control others. Sheldon (1992, 1997) reported that English-speaking girls typically master "double-voice" discourse, a type of conflict talk in which speakers make assertions while using conflict-mitigating strategies such as compromise, evasion, and clarification of intent. Efforts to avoid confrontation are made in line 6 'you do this, and I'll do this' and in lines 13 to 16, where Mika brings over another cutting board and knife and expresses concern regarding their appropriateness. Yukako compromises, saying she will use the small knife. Mika also uses evasion as a way to avoid conflict, by changing the subject (line 11). Using such tactics, the girls are able to find and agree on resolutions, maintaining overall group cohesion.

As seen in this dialogue, during peer play, girls tend to use gender-neutral linguistic forms, although they seem to often rely on a feminine conversational style (e.g., engaging in conflict with "double-voice discourse" rather than bald aggressiveness). In this activity, the girls are cooking busily, conducting a joint activity requiring cooperation and compromise (given the limited resources), unlike the boys' interactions in Dialogue 1, which centers on aggressive conflict and threats. It is important to note that in both dialogues, the style and forms used by the boys and girls are closely related to the nature of the interactional context.

Same-Sex Peer Play With Activity Setting Controlled

As researchers such as Thorne (1986) and Sheldon (1990) have stressed, situations constrain behavior. Girls' and boys' behavior might be more of a function of the particular context of their play activities than of intrinsic gender attributes. In this study, detailed analyses revealed that the differences between boys' and girls' speech were reduced considerably when comparisons were made within specific activities (e.g., lego construction, rough-and-tumble play, pretend play) with similar types of interactions. It is extremely difficult, however, to find comparable dialogues even within specific activity contexts. For example, the boys often ended up fighting, breaking, or throwing things, and sometimes the girls never actually began play (i.e., they spent more time setting up the play context itself). Let us compare two play scenarios with same-sex peers playing store, a relatively gender-neutral pretend play context, in a comparable manner.

DIALOGUE 3: Store scene with two boys (Ma, 5;3, and Hiro, 5;0). The boys plunge into the context of the play immediately, without negotiating roles, setting up props, and so on.

1 Hiro: kore mo da—kore mo.
           This too, and this. ((puts things in basket,
           approaching Ma, the storekeeper, with money in hand))
2 Ma: aa boku no mono, boku no.
           It's my money, mine.
           ((looking for own money, thinks Hiro took his money))
3 Hiro: omae koko ni aru daroo? baka funde doo surun da yo.
           Isn't yours here? Stupid, why are (you) stepping on
           it? ((laughing, pointing to money under Ma's foot))
4 Ma: chiki chiki chiki. hyaku kyuujuu-hyaku-en.
           Ring, ring, ring. One hundred ninety-hundred yen.
           ((ringing up items on cash register, followed by brief*

conversation with researcher regarding location of camcorder))

5 Hiro: uso!
No way!

6 Ma: hyaku nijuu-hyaku-en.
One hundred twenty-hundred yen.

7 Hiro: uso, hyaku sanjyuu-kyuu-en da ze.
No way, it's 139 yen.

8 Ma: hyaku kyuujuu-kyuu-en
199 yen ((listing prices for various items))

9 Hiro: hai.
Here. ((giving Ma some money))

10 Ma: hyaku sanjyuu-kyuu-en, hyaku-kyuuju - hyaku-kyuuju roku-man-en.
139 yen, 190 - 1,960,000 yen.

11 Hiro: hai.
Here. ((giving Ma more money))

12 Ma: hyaku-kyuuju - hyaku-kyuuju-roku-man-en dakara zenbu choodai.
It's 190 - 1,960,000 yen so give it all to me.
((taking all of Hiro's money))

13 Hiro: zurui zo, omae wa!
You're unfair!

14 Ma: moo nai no?
(You) don't have any more?

15 Hiro: kono yaroo! kore yannai no, kotchi?
You jerk! ((hits Ma on the head, then changes subject, looking at cash register)) *Aren't (you) going to do this, this one?* ((referring to the cash register))

16 Ma: hai.
Here. ((passing change to Hiro))

17 Hiro: arigatoo.
Thank you.

18 Ma: chiki chiki chiki. ichi-en, ni-en:
Ring, ring, ring. One yen, two yen:

19 Hiro: usso! konna ni takakunee yo.
No way! (It's) not this expensive.

20 Ma: ni-en desu ne. shoo ga nai desu ne: °maa-kun wa demo konna ni ippai aru.°

It's two yen. It can't be helped, can it? But I have
lots (of money). ((in a low voice, to self))
((After brief aside with his mother, Hiro starts
putting things in the basket again))

21 Ma: doroboo da!
           Thief!
22 Hiro: hitotsu dake ni suru yo.
           (I'll) just take one.
23 Ma: okane o kurenai to dame desu.
           (You) must give me money.
24 Hiro: ee?
           what?
25 Ma: okane o kurenai to dame desu.
           (You) must give me money.
26 Hiro: ee?
           what?
27 Ma: OKANE O KURENAI TO DAME DESU!
           (You) must give me money!
28 Hiro: hai.
           Okay.
29 Ma: sore de ii ko desu.
           You are a good boy. ((speaking to him like a child))
           ((Hiro does not have any money, so he needs to get
           some money from Ma to pay for the items))
30 Hiro   bakayaroo hayaku kane choodee yo. kane hayaku kure yo.
           You stupid idiot hurry up and give me (the) money.
           Give the money to me quickly.
31 Ma: kane?
           Money? ((cocks his head to one side))
32 Hiro: un.
           Right.
33 Ma: °wakarimashita yo.° HAI, ICHI-EN!
           (I) understand. ((reluctantly)) *HERE, ONE YEN!*
34 Hiro: IYA DA!
           NO!
35 Ma: tokubetsu da zo! tokubetsu ni go-hyaku-en desu!
           This is special! (I'll) give you 500 yen as a favor!
36 Hiro: iya. (.) aa ii yo, ii yo.
           No! (.) okay, okay.

Both boys clearly are able to use masculine linguistic forms, even in this play context that does not call for bald aggressiveness. First, the boys were able to use gender-appropriate first-person pronouns, such as *boku* 'I' in line 2. They also were able to use gender-appropriate second-person pronouns, namely *omae* 'you' in lines 3 and 13. *Omae* is a casual way for boys to refer to one another. Second, they were able to use a variety of masculine sentence-final particles, namely *zo* (lines 13 and 35). In both cases, the use of *zo* is emphatic, making the statement a strong assertion, as in "I tell you" or "believe me." Hiro also uses *ze* in line 7. *Ze,* like *zo,* is emphatic and assertive but slightly more friendly. This particle often is used by men in informal contexts among friends or with listeners of lower status. Both children use *yo* (Hiro uses it six times), which is a particle used when the speaker is providing new information, while adding moderate emphasis. Although this particle is considered to be a gender-neutral sentence-final particle, it often is used when making claims, expressing opinions, or giving advice or warnings and therefore makes one seem authoritative or pushy if not mitigated by another sentence-final particle such as *wa* (light assertion) or *ne* (agreement). For example, in line 19, Hiro uses *yo* to challenge Ma about the price of his purchases. *Yo* also is used often with demands, as in line 30, or when giving permission, as in line 36.

There were also several examples of masculine lexical forms that could be described as slang or colloquial expressions, such as *yaroo* 'person' (line 15) and *bakayaroo* 'stupid' (line 30). Finally, there were also examples of nonstandard pronunciation in the form of phonological reductions, such as *yannai* for *yaranai* 'don't do' (line 15), *takakunee* for *takakunai* 'not expensive' (line 19), and *choodee* for *choodai* 'give me' (line 30).

In this scenario, there is absolutely no negotiation of roles, and the boys just plunge into the pretend play. The boy who happened to be holding the cash register at the time became the storekeeper, and the boy who did not became the customer. However, there is some discussion regarding role-appropriate behavior, as in line 15, when Hiro uses a question to ask Ma if he is going to use the toy cash register, and in line 23, when Ma uses the obligatory expression *-nai to dame* '(you) must' to insist that Hiro, the customer, must pay for the merchandise. In addition, Hiro constantly challenges Ma's expertise as a storekeeper by challenging him on prices (e.g., using the assertive sentence-final particle *ze* to say that the merchandise is 139 yen instead of 190 yen in line 7, using direct commands such as *kane choodee yo* 'give me the money' and *hayaku kure yo* 'give it to me quickly' in line 30), but Ma also challenges him back. Hiro also belittles Ma by calling him names (e.g., *kono yaroo* 'you jerk' in line 15, *bakayaroo* 'stupid' in line 30). Silly episodes similar to the slapstick humor and naughtiness of the Chinese boys in the Kyratzis and Guo (1996) data also appear throughout this dialogue.

These boys negotiate and use questions and answers more than the pair of boys in the first superhero dialogue. An example of an extended negotiation begins in line 30, where Hiro demands that Ma give him change. Although at first (line 31), Ma pretends not to know what Hiro is talking about by bluffing, asking *kane?* 'money?,' in line 33, Ma acquiesces, saying *wakarimashita yo* '(I) understand,' giving in to Hiro's demand for change. Ma gives Hiro 1 yen in change, which is not enough to satisfy Hiro, as we see by his strong retort in line 34, *iya da!* 'no!' Then, Ma compromises by giving Hiro 500 yen in change, emphasizing that this is a special compromise by using the assertive masculine sentence-final particle *zo* in line 35. Initially, Hiro still seems dissatisfied by Ma's attempt at compromise, but then he quickly agrees with *ii yo, ii yo* 'okay, okay.'

Here is a conversation taken from a store pretend-play scenario that occurs between two girls, approximately the same age as the previous two boys.

DIALOGUE 4: Store scene with two girls (Ayano, 5;1, and Nayumi, 5;0). Setting up the store scenario:

1 Ayano: *janken shiyoo. janken shite sa: katta hoo ga o-miseya san ni shiyoo.*
             Let's do 'janken'. Let's do 'janken' and the one who wins will be the storekeeper.
2 Both: JAN-KEN-POI!
             Paper-scissors-rock! ((Ayano loses))
3 Ayano: sore ja ne: atashi kore ne.
             So then, this, I'll. . . .
4 Nayumi: chotto, narabete kara da yo.
             Hey, (we) have to line up things first.
5 Ayano: atashi kore-
             This, I'll-. ((picking up a small basket))
6 Nayumi: kore ni suru, koko no.
             (I'll) use this, this one. ((takes large one))

7 Ayano: dame kore!
            No, this one! ((referring to the small one))
8 Nayumi: sore ja ikko shika kaenai yo.
            Then you can only buy one.
9 Ayano: iku yo!
            Here (I) go! ((attempting to start playing))
10 Nayumi: mada da yo. hai, okane-
            (I'm) not ready. Here, the money-
            ((giving Ayano some toy money))
11 Ayano: ee?
            Huh?
12 Nayumi: okane da yo, sore.
            That's the money.
13 Ayano: doko ni haitteta?
            Where was it?
14 Nayumi: konnaka.
            In here. ((pointing to bag))
15 Ayano: nantoka nantoka no okaeshi desu to ka iun ja nai?
            *Aren't (you) supposed to say "here's your change of
            so-and-so much?"* ((Nayumi continues to line up objects
            on table while Ayano waits))
16 Ayano: hayaku, hayaku.
            Hurry, hurry. ((stomping on ground impatiently))
17 Nayumi: dondon shicha ikemasen.
            (You) mustn't stomp.
18 Ayano: koko wa watashi no ouchi nan dakara . . . o-miseya-san wa
            koko.
            This is my house over here. The store is over here.
            ((Drawing line with foot. Nayumi picks up green toy
            and shows it to Ayano.))
19 Ayano: mame da- mame.
            It's a bean, a bean. ((Nayumi puts it in her mouth.))
20 Ayano: dame da yo- tabecha. dame da yo- kaeshinasai!
            (You) mustn't eat it. Don't! Give it back (to me).
            ((looking at objects on table))
21 Ayano: ironna mono ga aru ne.
            There are so many kinds of things, aren't there?
            ((Nayumi picks up a green bunch of grapes, then
            a purple bunch of grapes))

22 Nayumi: kore budoo janain da yo. masukatto- budoo da!
             kore wa koko deshoo.
             These aren't grapes. Muscat grapes-(these) are grapes!
             (I) should put this here, right ?

23 Ayano: doo demo ii kara hayaku!
             (I) don't care, just hurry up! ((impatiently))
             ((Nayumi arranges the rest of the store items))

24 Nayumi: *ii yo! hai!*
             Okay! I'm ready! Here! ((passing the large basket to
             Ayano))

25 Ayano: aru yo.
             (I) have (one). ((showing the small basket))

26 Nayumi: sore ja ikko shika kaenai yo.
             Then (you) can only buy one thing.

27 Ayano: ikko de ii no.
             One is fine. ((Puts the small one down and takes the
             large basket))

28 Nayumi: takai yo.
             (It's) expensive. ((referring to store items))

29 Ayano: takai?
             Expensive?

30 Nayumi: nani ni shimasu ka? jibun de suki na mono totte
             kudasai.
             What would (you) like? Please take whatever you like.

31 Ayano: kaki to:
             Persimmons and:

32 Nayumi: aisukuriimu wa ikaga?
             How about ice cream?

33 Ayano: un.
             Okay.

34 Nayumi: koko ni aisukuriimu arimasu yo.
             Here's the ice cream. ((Ayano brings basket to cash
             register.))

35 Nayumi: kore dake desu ka?
             Is this all?·

36 Ayano: hai.
             Yes.

37 Nayumi: go-hyaku-en desu.
             (It'll) be five hundred yen.
             ((continue to play))

Unlike the play scene with the two boys, Ayano and Nayumi hardly use any gender-based linguistic forms. The only form that they use consistently is the feminine first-person pronoun *atashi* in lines 3 and 5. They do not use any feminine sentence-final particles (i.e., *wa* for mild insistence or affective intensity and *kashira* for uncertainty). On the other hand, they also do not use any overtly masculine sentence-final particles, either. In general, they use gender-neutral sentence-final particles. For example, they frequently use *yo* to present new information (line 28), mark challenges (line 4), give opinions (lines 8 and 26), and give permission (line 24). They also use *ne* (line 21) to agree with each other and confirm shared information, and *no* to provide explanations in line 27.

The two girls start by drawing on a preestablished schema for store play and begin by assigning roles. The role of the storekeeper is the more desirable one, as the storekeeper gets to play with an attractive toy cash register. They use *janken,* or "paper-scissors-rock," to assign roles in the fairest manner possible.[9] They ask for each other's opinions (lines 21 and 22) and are able to use questions and answers both in role (e.g., lines 30–36) and out of role (e.g., lines 13–15).[10] They spend a great deal of time establishing the role-play setting, not just assigning roles, but also determining what each role entails (e.g., the storekeeper gives change) and setting up the physical setting (e.g., laying out the store items, determining the store boundaries) and props (e.g., figuring out which store basket to use).

Although the girls use language to create and maintain positions of closeness and equality, jointly constructing and establishing their pretend play schema, it is clear that they also are able to use language to make assertive moves, such as when negotiating roles (e.g., line 1), establishing the physical setting (e.g., line 18), and defining appropriate role behavior (e.g., lines 4, 15, 20). For example, Nayumi criticizes Ayano's impatient stomping on the ground as inappropriate behavior (line 17) by using the phrase -*te wa ikemasen* to mark prohibition, and in the next line, Ayano justifies her behavior as appropriate by providing an explanation, saying that she is stomping in her own house and not in the store. Similarly, in line 7, Ayano introduces conflict by directly challenging Nayumi's choice of the large basket as being the more appropriate prop for the shopping scenario by using the prohibition *dame kore!* 'no, this one!' as she presents the smaller basket. In line 8, Nayumi consequently uses the assertive sentence-final particle *yo* to argue that with the smaller basket, Ayano will only be able to buy one item. Ayano also expresses her impatience with Nayumi's leisurely arrangement of the store items by using direct commands, such as *hayaku, hayaku* 'hurry, hurry' in line 16 and *doo demo ii kara hayaku!* '(I) don't care, just hurry up!' in line 23. Such assertive and controlling speech acts resemble those found in the boys' peer interactions in Dialogues 1 and 3 and show that, depending on the nature of the interactional context and the manner in which the children interact in the context, girls are just as capable of making assertive, coercive moves as boys are. Such data challenge traditional views that claim that girls are less assertive and more harmonious, and that boys are more "forceful" or "coercive" in pursuing their own agendas (e.g., Miller, Danaher, & Forbes, 1986; Sachs, 1987; Sheldon, 1992).

DISCUSSION

Peers are a crucial source of language socialization, particularly regarding gender-appropriate language use (e.g., Sachs, 1987; Sheldon, 1990). Even the youngest children showed a high level of metalinguistic awareness and were quick to correct their peers when gender-inappropriate language forms were used. In fact, in general, they were more likely to correct their peers for gender-inappropriate language than their mothers were. Examples of both boys and girls correcting their peers for gender-inappropriate language were observed.[11] For example, a 4-year-old girl, Rina, was criticized by her peers during snacktime for saying *umai naa!* '(this is) delicious!,' using the masculine lexical form for 'delicious,' which her female peers immediately rejected as gender inappropriate.[12] Similarly, a 3-year-old boy, Kosuke, often is teased by his male peers for using the feminine sentence-final particle *wa,* which he probably uses because he spends a majority of his time with his mother and female peers. Peers often assure the observance of gender-stereotyped norms by teasing and taunting the child who fails to conform.

In interviews with the mothers of the target children, it was clear that all of the mothers believed that peers were a powerful form of influence regarding their children's use of language. The mothers commented that their children's language changed in various ways as they spent more of their time in peer groups. In general, mothers of boys agreed that their sons' language became more rough after they entered preschool and spent more time in same-sex peer groups, playing with other boys. This was especially true in the case of only children and eldest children, who had limited exposure to masculine linguistic forms (e.g., only from fathers, television) prior to preschool.

In addition, some mothers of girls also commented that their daughters' language became more masculine and rough after they entered preschool, with increased exposure to boys' speech during mixed-sex peer play. In fact, several of the girls went through a brief phase in which they frequently used gender-inappropriate masculine linguistic forms, much to the disappointment of their parents.

All of the children were able to use a variety of gender-based linguistic forms in their same-sex peer play. When engaging in same-sex peer play, boys tended to use masculine linguistic forms (as compared to when they were playing with their mothers), whereas girls tended to use gender-neutral forms for the most part, with a smattering of feminine linguistic forms.[13] Furthermore, children often adopted a conversational style that matched their sex. In general, boys often used commands and challenges, whereas girls often used questions, explanations, requests for opinions and permission, and mitigated and indirect requests. In this respect, they were similar to the American girls and boys of previous studies, in which boys used language "assertively," whereas girls used language to mark cooperation and collaboration (e.g., Kyratzis & Guo, 1996; Maltz & Borker, 1982; Sheldon, 1990). Girls were able to negotiate to enhance communication and respond to the needs of others using various tactics such as compromise, clarification of intent, and evasion to mitigate opposition. As found by Sheldon (1992), the girls jointly constructed and maintained their pretend play, whereas the boys tended to use heavy-handed strategies such as threats and physical force. Silly and naughty behavior, as well as challenges and conflicts, marked their dialogues, and their pretend scenarios did not develop very much.

This does not mean that boys exclusively used commands and challenges or that girls always used mitigated language. Boys and girls were capable of using different linguistic forms, depending on the nature of the interactional context. Gender differences in communicative style were reduced greatly when comparisons were made within specific activity types and interactional contexts. Girls could be assertive and rough when fighting or when engaging in rough-and-tumble play, using some masculine linguistic forms and a more masculine communicative style.[14] In general, it was more difficult to get boys to use feminine style with their same-sex peers (although some were willing to do this when role playing with their mothers). When comparisons were made within specific activity contexts, differences were reduced. For example, in Dialogues 3 and 4, both pairs of children were engaged in a shopping scenario, which required extensive negotiation tactics (e.g., regarding the reciprocal, complementary roles of shopkeeper and customer, allocation of props). While playing store, the boys used fewer challenges and commands, as well as fewer threats and less physical force, than they usually used during superhero pretend play or rough-and-tumble play. Similarly, the girls in Dialogue 4 focused their attention on negotiation roles (e.g., deciding on who plays the customer and who plays the shopkeeper, determining what each role entails, establishing the setting for the scenario) and varied their linguistic strategies to negotiate in the most effective manner possible, by using questions and answers, agreeing with each other, confirming shared information, and presenting new information. At the same time, the girls in Dialogue 4 were able to use linguistic devices to mark assertive moves in their negotiations. It is important to note that Japanese boys' and girls' communicative styles are far from distinct; in other words, there is considerable overlap in their discourse styles. Gender-distinctive language is not a fixed, cross-situational individual trait, but rather something that occurs in the context of particular types of social interactions and relationships.

Therefore, it is obvious that language should not be labeled "feminine" or "masculine," suggesting that boys and men use only one form and girls and women use another. Regarding gender differences in language use, both stereotyping and overgeneralization must be avoided. Researchers such as Goodwin (1980, 1988), Thorne (1986), and Sheldon (1990, 1997) argue that gendered talk is situationally dependent and raise the need to be sensitive to differences in context (e.g., setting, topic, activity, listener characteristics). Therefore, in determining gender differences in children's language use, it is clear that we must pay close attention to the nature of the play context. The data show that even young children are able to vary language according to the "stance" that they are trying to "project" to others in a given context (Ochs, 1993). Similarly, children (both boys and girls) attempted to be aggressive and forceful during rough-and-tumble play or superhero pretend scenarios, marking their speech with challenges, conflict, and heavy-handed threats, whereas both boys and girls were more likely to use negotiation tactics in their roles as storekeeper–customer in shopping scenarios or extended questions and explanations and polite language in their roles as doctor–patient in hospital scenarios. Therefore, overall, when boys' and girls' language are compared within a given interactional context, gender-based linguistic differences are reduced drastically. Clearly, we need to study the discourse of children in a wide variety of natural situations, with different interactants, to see how children vary their usage of gender-based linguistic forms and communicative styles according to different contextual factors (Sheldon, 1997).

However, it must be noted that in the case of Japanese children, some robust gender-based linguistic differences remain, even when comparisons were made within a given interactional context. In other words, we need to distinguish between the linguistic features most closely tied to the speaker's gender identity as male or female (i.e., linguistic features that are used all the time) and those that relate to specific role-situational constraints to be socially masculine or feminine (i.e., linguistic features that vary according to one's stance as influenced by contextual and situational constraints; Kitagawa, 1977). For example, even when girls are engaged in rough-and-tumble play in an aggressive manner, they do not use masculine first-person pronouns such as *ore* and *boku,* although they might use masculine sentence-final particles such as *zo* and *ze.* This occurs because some gender-based linguistic forms seem to be linked more closely to the fixed gender identity of the speaker than others, and incorrect use of some linguistic forms is more marked than incorrect use of others.[15] For example, for many Japanese children, use of gender-appropriate first-person pronouns (i.e., *boku* and *ore* for boys, *atashi* for girls in casual conversation) seems to be tied closely to the biological sex of the child, whereas use of gender-based sentence-final markers seems to be related more to the stance that the child wants to project within an interactional context (e.g., use of assertive markers such as *zo* and *ze* and slang by boys and girls in rough play). Although use of some gender-based linguistic markers (e.g., sentence-final particles, nonstandard pronunciation, masculine or feminine lexical choices) varies according to the nature of the context and the types of interactional moves that make up each individual context (e.g., negotiation, conflict, agreement), use of other gender-based linguistic markers (e.g., using masculine as opposed to feminine first-person pronouns) varies less according to context. Shibamoto (1985), based on a study of the speech of two young male transvestites, concludes that some features of speech can be manipulated consciously, whereas it is difficult to manipulate others.

The issue of individual differences also must be taken into consideration. For example, whereas older Japanese women might never use masculine first-person pronouns such as *ore* and *boku,* even in marked contexts, recently teenage girls are less hesitant about using such forms in certain contexts. Trendy junior high school and high school girls in urban areas also can be heard using masculine sentence-final particles such as *zo, ze,* and *na*; non-standard pronunciation; and slang in their daily conversations (e.g., Okamoto, 1995). Standards regarding gender-appropriate usage of linguistic forms are changing constantly. Some individual differences stem from generational and regional differences in language usage (e.g., women in rural areas use fewer gender-based linguistic markers in general), as well as differences in educational background and social class (e.g., Kitagawa, 1977). Other individual differences are more personal, having to do with interactional style and personality, and the stances that each individual attempts to project in different contexts. For example, based on the language of the four boys in two of the scenarios presented earlier, it is apparent that Hiro's and Ryota's linguistic and interactional styles are more rough and aggressive (e.g., more direct imperatives, more challenges) than those of Ma and Masaki.

Individual differences also are apparent in other aspects. Although it can be said that the majority of the target children preferred to play with same-sex friends, two of the target children consistently preferred to play with opposite-sex friends. It was clear that some of the children who preferred to play in mixed-sex dyads showed different patterns of language use (e.g., a 3-year-old boy who preferred to play with girls sometimes used the feminine sentence-final particle *wa,* a 5-year-old girl who preferred to play with boys frequently used masculine linguistic forms). Clearly, more research needs to be conducted on language use in mixed-sex dyads and friendship groups.[16] Furthermore, data from boys or girls with minimal contact with same-sex peers (e.g., boys who do not attend preschool, girls with older brothers who prefer to play with boys), namely data from children who do not follow the norms of their peer culture in terms of gender-appropriate behavior and language, also would help to provide insight regarding different patterns of language and gender socialization. Such children often use linguistic features traditionally associated with the opposite sex, but it is important to note that their language is also influenced strongly by their exposure to factors such as siblings, parents, and television.

CONCLUSIONS

The results of this study show that peers serve as critical agents of gender socialization, particularly regarding language. This also has been found to be true for English-speaking children (e.g., Goodwin, 1980;

Kyratzis & Guo, 1996; Sheldon, 1990) and points to the need for more research on language and peer interaction. In the case of Japanese children, this is especially true for boys, who receive much of their input regarding gender-appropriate discourse and patterns of interaction from other boys. However, it also was discovered that contextual factors (e.g., play activity, hearer characteristics such as gender) play a key role in the selection and use of gender-based linguistic forms and communicative styles, and that children are sensitive to such factors from as early as age 3. For example, when comparisons were made within a given type of play activity (assuming that the types of interactions within the play activity were comparable), gender differences in language use were reduced considerably (e.g., use of specific gender-based sentence-final particles). Individual differences also appeared, with different children using gendered language to different degrees in different contexts.

However, it is also important to note that in the case of Japanese, gender differences were not eliminated completely, even when comparisons were made within specific contexts, as use of some gender-appropriate forms such as first-person pronouns remained relatively consistent across contexts. In other words, although some linguistic forms varied greatly according to the gender stance of the child in a given situational context, with gender being constantly negotiated, other linguistic forms were less variable and seemed to be tied more closely to the child's own gender identity.

NOTES

1   As mentioned in the introduction to this issue, it is important to note that traditional views of gender that treat gender in terms of dichotomous, polar differences currently are being revised. Recent work by various researchers, such as Sheldon's (1992, 1997) work on "double-voice discourse," shows how girls' competitive and adversarial behaviors often co-occur with cooperation and mitigation. This issue is discussed later.

2   Please refer to Nakamura (1997b) for a comprehensive review of the literature on gender socialization in Japan as well as in Western cultures.

3   Feminine sentence-final particles such as *wa* and *kashira* mark light assertion and uncertainty, respectively, whereas masculine sentence-final particles such as *zo* and *ze* mark strong assertion. It also must be noted that many sentence-final particles are gender neutral.

4   Sino-Japanese compound words (*kango*) were borrowed from China in approximately the 5th century A.D. These words were written in *kanji* (Chinese characters) and

"were heavily concentrated in the political, religious, economic, and scholarly domains, where the Japanese lexicon had no native terms available for many new objects and activities" (Shibamoto, 1985, p. 161). These areas were dominated by men, and only men were allowed to write *kanji*. Shibamoto claimed that this influenced the use of *kango* by women in both written and verbal expression. Women often avoid usage of *kango*, which are characterized as "difficult" and, therefore, "unfeminine."

5   Of course, these results are only valid for this set of participants, as toy preference was influenced by the selection of toys provided by the researcher. Total time was approximately 20 hr for each age group. Each of the 12 boys and 12 girls (8 in each age group) were visited once a month, and these data are taken from their peer interactions.

6   The system of romanization used in the transcripts is the Hepburn system, and the transcripts have been prepared according to the Jeffersonian system (except that underlining has been used to highlight gender-based linguistic features).

7   Ryota's threat to spank Masaki is an example of one of the silly and naughty acts that often appear in Japanese boys' peer play. Such behavior is similar to that which appears in the play of Chinese 5-year-old boys (Kyratzis & Guo, 1996).

8   Work on phonological variation in English-speaking children also illustrates that gender differences are present from an early age (e.g., Fischer, 1958). Japanese men often use nonstandard variants in the form of phonological reductions during informal speech, which often have a derogatory connotation, whereas Japanese women are more likely to use phonetic forms that more closely approach the standard language or have higher prestige (Ide, 1990).

9   Refer to Sachs (1987) for a description of the similar manner in which English-speaking boys and girls assign roles.

10 In this case, it often is possible to tell whether Nayumi is in role or out of role according to her use of polite language (e.g., use of formal *masu* verb endings, polite request forms). For example, when assuming the role of the storekeeper in lines 34, 35, and 38, Nayumi uses formal *-masu* verb endings but uses informal *-da* verb endings when out of role (e.g., lines 22, 24, 26). In general, both Japanese boys and girls are able to conduct simple pretend-play register shifts even before age 3, marking specific roles by varying politeness and formality levels, and using gender-appropriate linguistic forms (Nakamura, 1997b).

11 During the 40 hr of recorded peer interactions, there were approximately 30 examples of peers correcting peers' gender-inappropriate language use. This was close to 90% of the total number of times in which the children used obvious gender-inappropriate forms.

12 Of course, it is possible that Rina is speaking in out-of-role talk for just this one utterance, assuming the role of a boy, but her friends are so shocked by the use of this rough language that they immediately reject it.

13 Girls did use feminine linguistic forms when engaged in role play, especially when assuming the roles of older women. The use of gender-neutral language by the girls

reflects the frequent use of gender-neutral forms by their mothers in their daily interactions with their children and surrounding adults.

14 However, overall, there were few episodes of rough-and-tumble play and physical fighting in the girls' data. The few incidents that were recorded were brief in length and were terminated quickly by adult intervention (i.e., adults seemed to be more tolerant of rough-and-tumble play and physical fighting in boys' peer interactions).

15 However, this also varies according to the individual. For example, Ogawa (1999), in her study of gay male speech, reported that some gay male speakers use both masculine and feminine first-person pronouns, depending on the context, pointing to the fluid dynamicity of gender.

16 Thorne (1993) argued that "separate worlds" is not the reality for all children, as some children do not prefer to play in same-sex friendship groups.

REFERENCES

Bandoo, M. (1998). *Nihon no josei deetabanku* [Japanese women's databank]. Tokyo: Ministry of Finance Publishing.

Block, J. H. (1983). Differential premises arising from differential socialization of the sexes: Some conjectures. *Child Development, 54,* 1335–1354.

Fischer, H. K. (1958). Social influences in the choice of a linguistic variant. *Word, 14,* 47–56.

Goodwin, M. (1980). Directive-response sequences in girls' and boys' task activities. In S. McConnell-Ginet, R. Borker, & N. Furman (Eds.), *Women and language in literature and society* (pp. 157–173). New York: Praeger.

Goodwin, M. (1988). Co-operation and competition across girls' play activities. In A. D. Todd & S. Fisher (Eds.), *Gender and discourse: The power of talk* (pp. 55–94). Norwood, NJ: Ablex.

Ide, S. (1979). Person references of Japanese and American children. *Language Sciences, 1,* 273–293.

Ide, S. (1990). How and why do women speak more politely in Japanese. In S. Ide & N. H. McGloin (Eds.), *Aspects of Japanese women's language* (pp. 63–79). Tokyo: Kuroshio Shuppan.

Imamura, A. (1993). Interdependence of family and education: Reactions of foreign wives of Japanese to the school system. In J. Shields (Ed.), *Japanese schooling: Patterns of socialization, equality and social control* (pp. 16–27). University Park, PA: Penn State University Press.

Inoue, T., & Ehara, Y. (1995). *Josei no deetabukku* [Women's databook]. Tokyo: Yuhikaku.

Kitagawa, C. (1977). A source of femininity in Japanese: In defense of Robin Lakoff's *Language and woman's place. Papers in Linguistics, 10,* 275–298.

Kyratzis, A., & Guo, J. (1996). "Separate worlds for girls and boys?" Views from U.S. and Chinese mixed-sex friendship groups. In D. I. Slobin, J. Gerhardt, A. Kyratzis, & J. Guo (Eds.), *Social interaction, social context, and language: Essays in honor of Susan Ervin-Tripp* (pp. 555–577). Mahwah, NJ: Lawrence Erlbaum Associates, Inc.

Maccoby, E. (1988). Gender as a social category. *Developmental Psychology, 24,* 755–765.

Maccoby, E. (1990). Gender and relationships: A developmental account. *American Psychologist, 45,* 513–520.

Maltz, D. N., & Borker, R. A. (1982). A cultural approach to male–female miscommunication. In J. H. Gumperz (Ed.), *Language and social identity* (pp. 196–216). Cambridge, England: Cambridge University Press.

Miller, P., Danaher, D., & Forbes, D. (1986). Sex-related strategies for coping with interpersonal conflict in children aged five and seven. *Developmental Psychology, 22,* 543–548.

Nakamura, K. (1997a). Gender-based differences in the language of Japanese preschool children: A look at metalinguistic awareness. In E. V. Clark (Ed.), *The proceedings of the 28th Child Language Research Forum* (pp. 213–222). Palo Alto, CA: Center for the Study of Language and Information.

Nakamura, K. (1997b). *The acquisition of communicative competence by Japanese children: The development of sociolinguistic awareness.* Unpublished doctoral dissertation, University of California, Berkeley.

Ochs, E. (1993). Indexing gender. In B. D. Miller (Ed.), *Sex and gender hierarchies* (pp. 146–169). Cambridge, England: Cambridge University Press.

Ogawa, N. (1999, August). *Genderly speaking: Linguistic indexing choices.* Paper presented at the 12th World Congress of Applied Linguistics, Tokyo.

Okamoto, S. (1995). "Tasteless Japanese": Less "feminine" speech among young Japanese women. In K. Hall, M. Bucholtz, & B. Moonwomon (Eds.), *Locating power: Proceedings of the Second Berkeley Women and Language Conference* (pp. 478–488). Berkeley, CA: Berkeley Women and Language Group.

Okubo, A. (1967). *Yooji gengo no hattatsu* [The development of child language]. Tokyo: Tokyodoo.

Paley, V. G. (1984). *Boys & girls: Superheroes in the doll corner.* Chicago: University of Chicago Press.

Peak, L. (1991). *Learning to go to school in Japan: The transition from home to preschool life.* Berkeley: University of California Press.

Rheingold, H. L., & Cook, K. V. (1975). The content of boys' and girls' rooms as an index of parents' behavior. *Child Development, 46,* 459–463.

Sachs, J. (1987). Preschool boys' and girls' language use in pretend play. In S. Philips, S. Steele, & C. Tanz (Eds.), *Language, gender and sex in comparative perspective* (pp. 178–188). Cambridge, England: Cambridge University Press.

Sakata, M. (1990). The acquisition of Japanese "gender" particles. *Language and Communication, 11(3),* 117–125.

Sato, Y. (1977). *Onna no ko wa tsukurareru* [Women are created]. Tokyo: Shiraishi Shoten.

Sheldon, A. (1990). Pickle fights: Gendered talk in preschool disputes. *Discourse Processes, 13*, 5–31.

Sheldon, A. (1992). Conflict talk: Sociolinguistic challenges to self-assertion and how young girls meet them. *Merrill-Palmer Quarterly, 38*, 95–117.

Sheldon, A. (1997). Talking power: Girls, gender, enculturation and discourse. In R.Wodak (Ed.), *Gender and discourse* (pp. 225–244). London: Sage.

Shibamoto, J. S. (1985). *Japanese women's language*. New York: Academic.

Shimizu, K., Akao, K., Arai, A., Ito, M., Sato, H., & Yaosaka, O. (1996). *Kyooiku deetaarando '96–'97* [A databook of educational statistics '96–'97]. Tokyo: Jiji Tsuushinsha.

Takahashi, I. (1969). *Yooji no gengo to kyooiku* [The language and education of young children]. Tokyo: Kyooiku Shuppan.

Tannen, D. (1990). *You just don't understand: Women and men in conversation*. New York: Morrow.

Thorne, B. (1986). Girls and boys together . . . but mostly apart: Gender arrangements in elementary schools. In W. Hartup & Z. Rubin (Eds.), *Relationships and development* (pp. 167–184). Hillsdale, NJ: Lawrence Erlbaum Associates, Inc.

Thorne, B. (1993). *Gender play: Girls and boys in school*. New Brunswick, NJ: Rutgers University Press.

Tobin, J., Wu, D. Y. H., & Davidson, D. H. (1989). *Preschool in three cultures*. New Haven, CT: Yale University Press.

Whiting, B. B., & Edwards, C. P. (1988). *Children of different worlds: The formation of social behavior.* Cambridge, MA: Harvard University Press.

Yamamoto, M. (1997). *Gendai no wakai hahaoya-tachi* [Contemporary young mothers]. Tokyo: Shinyoosha.

Research on Language and Social Interaction, 34(1), 45–74

Preschool Girls' and Boys' Verbal Conflict Strategies in the United States and China

Amy Kyratzis
Graduate School of Education
University of California, Santa Barbara

Jiansheng Guo
School of Psychology
Victoria University of Wellington
and
Department of Human Development
California State University, Hayward

Although a wide body of research on sex–gender differences with White middle-class children in the United States has supported the separate worlds hypothesis (SWH), research with children from other cultures, including Taiwan, and Latino and African American children in the United States have challenged the view of girls' language as cooperative. In this study, we examine the linguistic strategies by which middle-class girls and boys from the United States and Mainland China manage conflict. Preschoolers were videotaped playing with peers. In same-sex groupings, Chinese girls and U.S. boys used the most direct strategies, including

The American research reported was supported by a grant entitled "Gender, Peer Groups, and Social Identity in the Preschool" to Amy Kyratzis from the Spencer Foundation. Collection, transcription, and analysis of the Chinese data were supported by three Internal Research Grants from the Science Faculty of Victoria University of Wellington. We are grateful to the children who participated in the two studies and their parents, teachers, and school administrators. We gratefully acknowledge Amy Sheldon and Karen Tracy for comments on earlier drafts.

Correspondence concerning this article should be sent to Amy Kyratzis, Graduate School of Education, University of California, Santa Barbara, CA 93106. E-mail: Kyratzis@education.ucsb.edu third-party complaints and censures and aggravated commands. Chinese boys used a combination of direct and indirect conflict strategies. U.S. girls used the most mitigated strategies. The pattern found in the United States of boys being more assertive than girls supported the SWH, whereas the pattern found in China was the reverse. Possible explanations of this cultural difference are provided. In cross-sex conflict in both cultures, girls dominated in some contexts but not others, suggesting contextual complexity in the consequences of conflict strategies. Results challenge the portrait of girls' language that the SWH and other gender–language models have posited.

A wide body of research on sex–gender differences with White middle-class children in the United States has supported the separate worlds hypothesis (SWH; Maltz & Borker, 1982; Tannen, 1990). However, studies examining children's talk in other cultures, including research with African American and Latino American children in the United States (Goodwin, 1990a, 1990b, 1995) and studies with Chinese-speaking preschoolers in Taiwan (Farris, 1991, 1999, in press) and Mainland China (Kyratzis & Guo, 1996), have found that girls as well as boys engage well in conflict and assertive speech. These cultural differences are consistent with Ochs's (1992) claim that we should think of gender as constituted at least partly by the relations of language to culture-specific "stances" or general interaction poses having to do with how one presents oneself to others. Perhaps assertiveness is a stance valued for girls in some cultures but not in others. According to feminist researchers (Bing & Bergvall, 1996; Cameron, 1996), such cultural differences are important to examine as they argue against the universalism inherent in the SWH and other dichotomous approaches to gender and language.

In this article, we undertake a comparative study examining the discursive strategies by which girls and boys negotiate conflict in two cultures: the United States and Mainland China. Based on past research (Farris, 1991, 1999, in press; Kyratzis & Guo, 1996), China represents an especially interesting contrast with the United States. Unlike their U.S. counterparts, Chinese preschool-age girls have been observed to be quite assertive.

We begin by reviewing past research on the discursive practices by which children have been observed to manage conflict in the two cultures. Then, the study procedures in the United States and China are described. The analytic heart of the article is a description of same-sex and mixed-sex conflict strategies in the two cultures. Results from the same-sex conflict show that girls' cooperative language is far from being a universal characteristic. Results from the cross-sex conflict illustrate the contextual complexity of conflict strategies.

PAST STUDIES OF AMERICAN CHILDREN

Past research has portrayed a strong contrast between U.S. middle-class boys' and girls' strategies for managing conflict. For example, Sheldon (1990) found that American boys tended to use heavy-handed conflict tactics, including bald refusals ("No!") and escalation of conflict through insistence. In contrast, American girls were found to be under social constraints to "be nice" (Sheldon, 1992, 1996) and "say it with a smile" (Sachs, 1987), reflecting a relationship orientation. Even though American girls engaged in conflicts, they used "double-voice discourse," a highly assertive feminine conflict style that had an overlay of mitigation (Sheldon, 1992, 1996). Strategies of double-voicing included the "yes, but" strategy, a move that prefaces refusal with token agreement, and providing justifications for refusing (Sheldon, 1992, 1996). Additional indirect strategies of conflict management used by girls included ignoring, postponing (e.g., "You're the baby brother, but you aren't born yet"), and reframing a proposal without explicit refusal (Sheldon, 1996).

In contrast to these findings from middle-class U.S. children, Goodwin (1990a, 1990b, 1995) found that African American and Latina working-class girls in the United States did not use indirectness or mitigation for managing conflict. Instead, they used very direct "procedures to build opposition," including expressions of polarity (e.g., "No!" at the beginning of a turn), negative person descriptors, insult terms, disclaimers (e.g., "So?" and "I don't care!"), and discrediting stories. African American girls' discrediting stories revealed that these girls were not only as skilled in argumentation as boys, but also had more extended and more complex participant structures in their argumentation (Goodwin, 1990a, 1990b). Latina girls also were found to use direct strategies for building opposition in a game of hopscotch: expressions of polarity, response cries ("au:!" or "ou:!" to the offending actions), negative personal descriptors ("chillona" or "cheater"), and explication of previous oppositions ("hey!", then "you have to put yourself on this line with both feet very close together to the other foot girl!"; Goodwin, 1998, p. 39).

The contrast in conflict management strategies between White middle-class American girls on the one hand and Latina and African American girls on the other suggests that we cannot assume a set of conflict management strategies that apply to all girls or boys in general. Rather, attention has to be given to culture-specific strategies used by girls and boys.

PAST STUDIES OF CHINESE CHILDREN

Farris (1991, 1999), in an ethnographic study of peer language social-ization in a Mandarin Chinese-speaking preschool in Taiwan, found a complex pattern of conflict styles in same-sex and mixed-sex groups. Boys' conflict styles were direct. Boys used physical action (e.g., beating the air in front of a boy), teasing, insistence, and bald directives ("Bring a cup of coffee!").

In contrast, Taiwanese girls' conflict strategies could be either direct or indirect. In same-sex and mixed-sex groups, girls used indirect strategies such as reasoned argument, which sometimes involved rule invocations (e.g., "I won't give you coffee because this is not a store"; Farris, 1991, p. 209). Rule invocations are a type of adultlike posturing, and these girls also cited teacher authority to gain the upper hand in disputes. Girls also were found to use direct strategies, including bald directives, insults, and rhetor-ical questions used as complaints and censures delivered directly to the offending party ("How is it that you don't call others by name?" "What for do you scold others as pigs?"; Farris, 1991, p. 210). A particularly direct strategy involved censuring other girls by speaking about them in the third person in their presence (e.g., "As soon as one speaks to her, she sticks up her mouth. She thinks she is really great"; Farris, 1991, p. 209).

Kyratzis and Guo (1996) found that Mandarin-speaking preschool girls in Beijing, China, used highly assertive forms in conflict with boys. In one example, a girl in the role of the child was extremely authoritative with a boy in the role of father, repeatedly using direct and aggravated commands, such as *kuài* 'hurry,' making several critical comments (e.g., "What a lousy father you are"), and scolding and mocking the boy through rhetorical questions ("You simply give it to me to eat with detergent?"; Kyratzis & Guo, 1996, p. 571). Kyratzis and Guo suggested that the assertiveness of the Chinese girls might be context dependent, reflecting women's power and influence in the domestic domain. Farris (in press) made a similar argument for dual spheres of influence, with the observation that girls were silent in formal settings but "talkative and assertive" in informal ones, the former reflecting the role of "the virtuous wife" and the latter the role of the "good mother."

To summarize, past research suggests that Chinese middle-class girls might be socialized to use more assertive conflict strategies than American middle-class girls. This indicates that systematic cultural comparisons are important in understanding gender–language relations. We undertake such comparison in same-sex groups, where sociolinguistic styles are thought to be socialized. The past research on Chinese children also raises the issue of contextual specificity, including different gender compositions of a group. For that reason, this study expands our earlier (Kyratzis & Guo, 1996) comparison of Chinese and American girls' and boys' conflict strategies and systematically compares them in both same-sex and mixed-sex groups.

METHOD

The U.S. Study

The English data in this study came from two same-sex friendship groups, a girls' same-sex group and a boys' same-sex group. As part of a naturalistic observational study of gender and language socialization in nursery school friendship groups (Kyratzis, in press), friendship groups were identified and tracked over the course of 1 academic year. Preschool classes contained 16 children equally divided between girls and boys and 3- and 4-year-olds. Children were videotaped with their two most representative friendship groups at different points in the academic year.

There were 3 children in each of the two selected groups for this analysis: Rob, Paul, and John in the boys' group and Jenny, Peg, and Amy in the girls' group. All of the children but one were 4 years old at the time of the study. Two of the children were Asian American, one was Native American, and the remainder were European American. All were middle-class offspring of students, faculty, and staff of a university. The mixed-sex group consists of two of these girls (Jenny and Peg) who frequently played with a boy's group.

The Chinese Study

The Chinese data came from 3 girls and 3 boys in a university-based day care in Beijing, China (Guo, 1999). All of the children were 5-year-olds from middle-class families. They were from a senior class (*dàbān,* the highest of the three grades in the Chinese preschool system) of 33 children. They were selected with the help of the teacher on grounds of play compatibility and grouped into two same-sex triads and two mixed-sex triads.

Each triad was instructed to play with an elaborate Play-Doh machine in which Play-Doh could be placed and transformed into different shapes. This activity involves both a domestic play theme (making food with Play-Doh) and a technical theme (how to operate a machine), stereotypical girls' and boys' domains, respectively.

These sessions were transcribed by Jiansheng Guo using the Pinyin system of romanization. English translations are indicated in italics.

The Chinese study consists of arranged interactions, whereas the U.S. study consists of spontaneous classroom interactions. In China, adult-directed tasks are more common than free play, so arranged activities and groups approximate everyday settings. Despite different procedures, the combined study allowed us to examine language socialization in same-sex and mixed-sex groups and draw some conclusions about managing conflict in each culture.

CONFLICT AND CONFLICT STRATEGIES

We examine the linguistic strategies that children use to express and negotiate conflict. Conflicts were defined as instances where a child disagrees with a partner's proposal or wants to do something (gain access to play materials or a play episode) that is resisted or likely to be resisted by another child.

We looked at verbal strategies identified in past work to express and negotiate conflict. Mitigated or indirect strategies included reasoned argument, the "yes, but" tactic, postponement, and the reframing of pretense proposals. Aggravated or direct strategies included polarity markers ("No!") and other explicit opposition markers (e.g., "Hey!" as a response cry), insults and put-downs, aggravated commands, threats, rhetorical questions (e.g., "What for do you scold others as pigs?"), face-to-face censures and criticisms, and third-party censures and criticisms (i.e., censures and criticisms made to one person about another in the latter's presence).

CONFLICT STRATEGIES IN SAME-SEX GROUPS

American Girls' Conflict Strategies in All-Girl Groups

Excerpts 1–4 are conflicts from a long episode of play involving three girls: Jenny, Peg, and Amy. They are sitting in circle, outdoors. The excerpts illustrate that U.S. middle-class girls engage in conflicts and strive to maintain hierarchical forms of social organization. However, these girls use mitigated or indirect conflict management strategies.

The tone of these interactions is highly collaborative. The girls use mitigated forms to cast their proposals and ideas for the play. However, there are tense moments of incipient conflict. Conflict stems from two sources; Jenny appears to be keen on not being bested by Peg, and Peg appears to be keen on not having Jenny prefer Amy to her.

Excerpt 1 exemplifies Jenny's use of the mitigated strategy of reframing the play.

Excerpt (1)

1	Peg:	oh I'm batman's girlfriend.
2	Jenny:	I'm- I'm- I'm batman's girlfriend, too.
3	Peg:	we- we- we live in different houses. I have to visit
4		batman now.
5	Jenny:	I'm the baby kitty. and- I'm the baby kitty and you
6		are my owner.
7	Peg:	yeah.

In this episode, Jenny alters a frame that she seems unable to contribute to and control. In line 1, Peg suggests a batman's girlfriend script. In line 2, Jenny merely repeats what Peg said, suggesting she is unfamiliar with the script. In lines 3 and 4, Peg elaborates the script further. In line 5, instead of making a contribution, Jenny shifts the frame so that they are pretending to be an owner and a baby kitty. As excerpts 2 through 4 show, this a script Jenny can contribute to and control.

Excerpt 2 is another use of the mitigated strategy of reframing to avoid conflict.

Excerpt (2)

1 Peg: yeah. Amy sit right here, baby. So, I got a surprise
2   for you, baby kitty, kitty.
3 Jenny: pretend we're both baby kitties.
4 Peg: yeah.
5 Amy: m<u>e</u> and <u>you</u>.
6 Peg: An- baby, I got some surprise for you ⌈here?
7 Jenny: ⌊pretend pretend we're both
8   baby kitties.
9 Peg: ba::by. we're all babies here/ baby eat some livers.

In this episode, Jenny attempts to change a scenario that she herself created in Excerpt 1, whereby she is the baby kitty, whereas Peg is in the more powerful role of her owner. To do so, Jenny attempts, in line 3, to shift the frame and render Peg an equal by proposing "We're both baby kitties." This change of frame will preempt Peg's higher status role, but by using the mitigated or indirect strategy, a direct conflict is avoided. The opposition could have been stated more baldly ("You can't be the owner"). However, by using the reframing strategy, Jenny's challenge is so muted that Amy misinterprets Jenny to mean that she, rather than Peg, should be a baby kitty (line 5), and Jenny has to repeat herself in line 7 to make herself clear.

In Excerpt 3, Jenny, Peg, and Amy are all standing beside an outdoor play box, pretending to be baby kitties. Jenny and Peg each have pulled up some grass ("stems"), each wanting her own grass to be used as the kitties' candy. In this argument, mitigated conflict strategies can be seen in the use of mitigated protests, mollifying statements, "yes, but" statements, collaborative connectives, and a frame shift.

Excerpt (3)

1 Jenny: pretend these stems are our candy. ((holds up grass))
2 Peg: look it! these are flat! ((holds up her grass for Amy to inspect))
3 Jenny: pretend these stems are our candy. ((holds up her grass for
           Peg and Amy to inspect))
4 Peg: look it! these are flat! ((holds up her grass for Amy and Peg to
           inspect))

5	Peg:	oh. mine. ((in response to Amy's taking some grass from her)) you can get some from over here.
6	Jenny:	pretend the middle was your food. ((out of range))
7	Peg:	yeah. ((in camera range again, Jenny and Peg are kneeling side by side before bench inside play box. Jenny has the grass she'd designated in front of her. Peg's grass is in pile outside play box))
8	Jenny:	pretend the middle was your food. ((refers to bench))
9	Peg:	yeah. and that's a- that's a pile over there.
10		((referring to her grass outside play box))
11	Jenny:	and the middle of this spot is your potty.
12	Peg:	yeah. ((reaches and takes grass from in front of Jenny on bench)) I get those. I need those. And those.
13	Jenny:	no.
14	Peg:	those are marshmallows.
15	Jenny:	these are- pretend ( ) I mean pretend I'm the mommy.
16		pretend I'm the Mommy one and you both are the baby ones.

In lines 1 and 3, Jenny is insistent that her grass be used as the kitties' candy. In lines 2 and 4, Peg protests but does so tactfully, with mitigation. She renders her "stems" as more interesting, pointing out their flatness, in an attempt to get Jenny and Amy to use them. In line 6 (repeated in lines 8 and 11), after the situation has shifted to Jenny's advantage, with her grass being on the play box bench in front of her and Peg's grass being in a pile outside the play box, Jenny mollifies Peg for having her grass discounted by stating "pretend the middle was your food." This is a mollifier because it requests Peg to be content with having no food at all, merely a spot on the bench. In line 9, Peg protests, using the mitigated "yes, but" strategy. She indicates her own discarded flowers ("that's a—that's a pile over there") but prefaces this challenge with agreement ("yeah"). She also uses the collaborative connective "and," which, when compared to "but," appears to build on what the partner said before. In line 11, Jenny insists on her way but with mitigation, prefacing her challenge with the collaborative connective "and" and again casting it as a mollifier. When Peg stands up for herself in line 12, taking some of Jenny's grass and designating it as her own, she marks this challenge first with "yeah," using the "yes, but" strategy. Jenny first protests with "no" in line 13. However, she then (lines 15 and 16) resorts to her mitigated strategy of shifting the pretend frame so as not to let Peg have the advantage. She instantiates a frame whereby the mommy kitty scratches the baby kitties' backs before they go to bed (continued in Excerpt 4). In this way, she bypasses the food issue completely.

In Excerpt 4, Peg and Jenny use the mitigated strategies of questions, mollifiers, and mitigating verbs to express opposition.

Excerpt (4)

1	Jenny:	these are- pretend ( ) I mean pretend I'm the mommy.
2		pretend you both are the baby ones.
3	Peg:	pretend that's our bed.
4	Jenny:	yeah. and I rub your- and I rub your back.
5	Peg:	yeah. and then I wanna go to bed.
6	Jenny:	kitty, I'll rub the <u>other</u> kitty's back first.
7	Peg:	why?
8	Jenny:	Sue's back.
9	Peg:	why?
10	Jenny:	'cause Amy is- is nicer.
11	Peg:	no. I'm nicer to you too.
12	Jenny:	you're <u>both</u> nicer to me, so I'll rub <u>both</u> of your
13		backs.
14	Peg:	at the same time?
15	Jenny:	I think I have to rub <u>one</u> at a time and then I'll rub
16		yours second.
17	Peg:	okay. pretend it's nap time.

In this episode, Peg challenges Jenny's proposal in line 4 that she will rub the other kitty's (Amy) back first. She responds with a question ("why?"), a mitigated form of challenge, in lines 7 and 9. In line 11, Peg challenges Jenny's reason ("because Amy is nicer") with a protest that, unlike her usual style of conflict talk, explicitly marks the polarity ("no, I'm nicer to you too.") This prompts Jenny to use a joint directive ("both of you are nicer") and a statement that appears to be a compromise ("so I'll rub both your backs"). This statement is another mollifier. It accentuates the positive (that Peg's back will get rubbed) while avoiding mention of the negative (that Peg's back will not be rubbed first). Peg uses mitigated challenge, in question form, in line 14 ("at the same time?") In lines 15 and 16, Jenny counters this with a mitigated refusal without polarity markers and containing a mitigating verb ("I think I have to do one at a time") followed by a mollifier ("but I'll do yours second"). This statement attempts to mollify Peg for not getting all of what she wants by stating that she is getting part of what she wants. It is an artful form of double-voice discourse.

These excerpts show U.S. middle-class girls to be highly competitive and involved in arranging hierarchical forms of social organization. Jenny is locked in a struggle to maintain one-up status on Peg. Peg is locked in a struggle to maintain one-up status on Amy. However, the girls appear reluctant to express opposition, rarely using polarity markers. They also do not resort to threats or physical force. Through statements such as "We're both [meaning all] baby kitties" and "your food is in the middle here," as well as "I think I have to rub one at a time and then I'll rub yours second," the girls avoid direct opposition and mollify. The mollifying and masking statements highlight the positive and deemphasize the disagreement.

The mitigated conflict strategies displayed by these girls are consistent with those described by Sheldon (1992, 1996). Like Sheldon found, these girls used frame shifting to avoid conflict. In fact, frame shifting was even more prevalent in our data than what Sheldon found. We identified an additional tactic of mitigated conflict not previously described that we label the "mollifying statement." Mollifiers highlight what a participant is getting rather than what she is not (e.g., "your food is in the middle here"). They are similar to the "yes, but" strategy in highlighting the positive. However, unlike the "yes, but" strategy, they do not voice the negative at all. A final verbal strategy of mitigated conflict management identified here is the use of "and" to preface disagreements rather than "no" or "but." These prefaces mask the fact that any oppositional stance is being taken.

Chinese Girls' Conflict Strategies in All-Girl Groups

The next two excerpts illustrate that Mandarin-speaking Chinese girls in same-sex groups use very direct strategies of conflict management. They use various forms of censure, direct commands, threats, and even physical force. Their strategies show a sharp contrast to those of their U.S. middle-class counterparts but resemble in several ways those used by African American and Latina girls as reported by Goodwin (1990a, 1990b).

In this triad of girls, Fu and Sun frequently sided against Shi, and the disputes usually involved criticizing Shi for some fault in her character (being stubborn or greedy). Excerpt 5 illustrates an episode of conflict.

Excerpt (5)
Children = Shi (SH) = girl, Sun (SU) = girl, and Fu (FU) = girl

1　FU: 　((grabs toy knife next to SH and SU)) gěi wǒ zhèige!
　　　　Give it to me!

2   SH: ((closes lid of SU's box abruptly))
3   SU: ((while giggling, to SH accusingly))
4   SU: tǎoyànjìnr de, wǒ de fàn hú la, dǒng ma?
          You nuisance. My food is burning. Do you
          understand?
5   nǐ hái gěi wǒ mēn,
          You still continue to steam it
6   SU: nǐ yào mēn dào shénme shíhòu? á?
          When are you going to stop steaming it? Huh?
7   ((moves to other side of table, tries to open lid))
8   FU: ((to SU)) zhè shì nǐ zìjǐ de!
          This is your own!
9   SU: ((to FU)) wǒ zhīdào zhè shì wǒ zìjǐ de,
          I know this is my own.
10 SU: tā bǎ wǒ de fàn hái yào mēn,
          She still wants to continue steaming it.
11 SU: tā yào bǎ wǒ de fàn,
          She will make my food . . .
12 FU: mēn hú sǐ.
          Steam burnt to death.
13 SU: tā yào bǎ wǒ de fàn mēn hú sǐ,
          She wants to steam my food burnt to death.
14 SH: ((closes lid forcefully, smiles))
15 SU: ((returns to seat, to SH)) tǎoyàn. zhēn tǎoyàn.
          You nuisance. You real nuisance.
16 SU: ((opens lid, tries to get some food out))
17 SH: ((tries to close lid while SU's hand is still in box))
18 SU: tǎo yàn ba!
          Nuisance, you.
19 SH: āiya, lǎo kāi, guān zhe gàn má?
          But, why do you always open, close it?

The Chinese girls in this excerpt use highly assertive conflict strategies, such as aggravated commands, complaints and censures, mocking
rhetorical questions, insistence, and physical force. The dispute is over the
status of the lid of a pot. Sun wants it open, and Shi wants it closed. The
exchange opens with Fu's aggravated command ("Give it to me") and her
physical action of grabbing a knife away from Shi (line 1). Shi responds
with physical force. She closes Sun's pot lid abruptly (line 2). In the Unit-

ed States, physical force is a heavy-handed strategy mainly used by boys (Sheldon, 1990). Sun responds with, in turn, an insult, a direct complaint, and a rhetorical question. In line 4, she states "You nuisance. My food is burning. Do you understand?" The rhetorical question "Do you understand?" is insulting, challenging the addressee's intelligence. So too are the put-downs "annoying" and "nuisance." In line 5, she uses insistence, "you still continue to burn it," implying that Shi is morally intransigent. This criticism is strengthened by Sun's rhetorical question in line 6 ("When are you going to stop steaming it, huh?").

In lines 8 to 13, Sun shifts from direct complaint to third-party complaint. She makes complaints about Shi to Fu ("She still wants to continue steaming it. She will make my food steam burnt to death"). However, these third-party complaints are in the presence of the party being criticized. Therefore, they are highly aggravated acts. In line 15, Sun again uses the insult ("You nuisance"). Then, both parties resort to physical force (lines 16 and 17), with Sun trying to take things out of the pot while Shi tries to close the lid on her hand. Sun makes another insult in line 18 ("Nuisance, you"), after which Shi makes a counter accusation in the form of a rhetorical question in line 19 ("But why do you always open, close it") to claim that Sun deserves it. By casting the issue in general terms ("always"), she turns the dispute to one about Sun's moral character rather than the immediate actions at hand.

Excerpt 6 is a dispute between Fu and the marginalized girl Shi. Fu wants a piece of Play-Doh that Shi will not relinquish. Direct conflict strategies can be seen in the use of physical force, negative polarity markers, threats, direct complaints, and warnings.

Excerpt (6): FU = girl, SH = girl

1 FU: ((opens SH's Play-Doh lid, addresses SH))

2 FU: SH, wǒ néng yòng nǐ zhè diǎn ba?
    SH, can I use this piece of yours, OK?

3 SH: ((takes Play-Doh away from FU)) bù xíng de!
    It's not OK.

4 ((protesting)) bù xíng ma!
    No way.

5 FU: nàge, nǐ dōu yòng rénjiā de,
    That, you already used mine.

6 FU: rénjiā bù néng yòng nǐ de ya? (to SU) duì ba?
    How come that I can't use yours? Right?

7 SU: duì.
         Right.
8 SH: ((made mess of hand with Play-Doh, shows FU hand and
9   Play-Doh))
10 FU: ((takes Play-Doh from SH's hand)) gěi wǒ, gěi wǒ.
         Give it to me. Give it to me.
11 SH: ((shows Guo her hand)) ya ya, shūshu nǐ kàn!
         Oh uh! Uncle, look.
12 SU: ((to SH)) duì, nǐ dōu yòng rénjiā de,
         That's right. You already used others'.
13 SU: rénjiā jiù bù néng yòng nǐ de?
         How come that others can't use yours?
14 SH: ((to GUO)) āi yā ya.
         Oh uh.
15 FU: ràng nǐ zhīdào diǎn lìhài nǐ jiù zhīdào le,
         *Show you some force and you will be able to understand
         it.*
16 FU: hei hei. ((to SU)) duì ba?
         Hei hei. Right?
17 SU: xiǎoqìguǐ, yǐhòu rénjiā bù gěi nǐ yòng.
         Miser. Later on, people won't give you things either.

Fu opens the dispute with the physical move of opening Shi's pot lid,
though softening it with a permission request in line 2 ("Can I use this
piece of yours, OK?"). Shi responds with a negative polarity marker in
line 3: "It is *not* okay." In line 4, Shi further strengthens this refusal by
another negative polarity marker ("No way"). Fu responds to the refusal
by making a direct complaint followed by a rhetorical question ("You
already used mine. How come that I can't use yours?"). In addition, she
uses the ambiguous lexical marker *rénjiā* 'one' to refer to herself indirectly, formulating her censure as a generic rule.

In line 10, Fu uses a physical tactic, grabbing the Play-Doh from Shi's
hand. This act is accompanied by an aggravated command and insistence
("Give it to me. Give it to me"). In lines 12 and 13, Sun sides with Fu by
making an emphatic statement ("That's right") and reiterating Fu's earlier
direct complaint ("You already used others. How come that others can't
use yours?"). Fu threatens Shi in line 15 ("Show you some force and you
will be able to understand it") and seeks support from Sun in line 16
("Right?"). Sun ends the dispute with a warning or premonition, prefaced
with an insult in line 17 ("Miser. Later on, people won't give you things

either"). The warning uses the generic reference word "people," casting the consequence in broader, moral terms.

In sum, the conflict strategies of these Mandarin-speaking girls are very direct. They include direct polarity markers, various forms of censure (direct and third-party complaints, rhetorical questions, insulting names), direct commands, threats, and even physical force. Unlike their middle-class U.S. counterparts, these girls do not mask or downplay opposition but rather use very direct strategies that resemble in several ways those used by the African American and Latina girls described by Goodwin (1990a, 1990b).

American Boys' Conflict Strategies in All-Boy Groups

The following conflict segments are from an episode of play involving some real bees. Rob, one of the boys, makes up a game whereby the other two boys, Paul and John, stand on a rock and wait their turn for Rob to call them over to this area to search for bees. Rob designates for how high a count the other two can search for bees and whether or not they can step on any given bee. At points, when they come down, Rob opposes them, saying they should not because he did not "tell" them to or he had not "decided" they could. He uses verbs of telling, desire, and knowing to aggravate commands, as when a parent says "I *said* you couldn't go" and "I *decided* you can't go." Verbs of telling, desire ("I want"), and knowing heighten the imposition of commands (Ervin-Tripp & Gordon, 1984), and Rob uses these forms to express his opposition to the other boys' moves assertively.

In Excerpt 7, Rob argues with Paul and John, using aggravated commands, polarity markers, and other direct strategies.

Excerpt (7)

1 John: =I ( )
2 Paul: [no, I-] I did that one.
3 Rob: [(okay)?]
4 Paul: by myself.
5 Rob: Paul did it. Hey, no. stand back there (.)
6   and when I find a l- ((ushers them onto the rock))
7   (.) when I find a bee, I'll call someone to step- (.)
8   step on it, okay?

In this episode, Rob tells the two boys that one of them should step on the bee. They both make stepping moves over the (for the most part) mythical bees and then argue over who it was who stepped on a bee. Rob ultimately resolves the dispute. He says, "Paul did it," providing no evidence for his claim. This is nonreasoned opposition consistent with boys' heavy-handed conflict strategies (Sheldon, 1990). After this resolution, Paul and John are standing around in the area with bees, and in line 5, Rob opposes them, wanting them to get back on the rock. His opposition is stated clearly with a polarity marker and direct command ("No, stand back there"), followed with an aggravated command with a verb of saying ("When I find a bee, I'll call someone to step on it"). In other words, he is telling the boys that they cannot get off the rock because he has not yet "called" them down from it.

Excerpt 8 is a conflict where Paul encourages John to "rebel" against Rob by running off the rock, and Rob responds to the insurrection by making Paul "the boss."

Excerpt (8)

```
1    Paul:    ((turning to look at John)) I hope he picks me.
2    John:    (I should run away?)
3    Paul:    okay. do it. °do it. do it.° (.) please. I'll
4             be your best- ((John runs away. Rob looks after
5             him)) Margo. ((John comes back and stands on the
6             rock next to Paul))
7    Rob:     (    ) I said(.) um (.) <when Paul's on
8             that rock>, I want Paul to be the boss. (.) when
9             John gets off, I want you to listen to Paul,
10            okay? ((shaking his finger at John and Paul))
```

In this excerpt, Rob uses aggravated forms. In line 7, he uses the verb of telling ("I said") and physical gesture (shaking his finger at the two boys) to heighten his expression of opposition (I said when Paul's on that rock, I want you to listen to Paul). The verb phrase "I want" also heightens the opposition. In a similar exchange, Rob opposed John's taking a particular number of turns by saying "I *decided* John gets two."

Excerpt 9 is another example of these U.S. boys' direct conflict strategies.

Excerpt (9)

```
1    Paul:    I found one.
2    Rob:     where is it ? (let go? (.) ( ) ((walking
3             forward)) DO NOT STEP. get back on the
```

4   rock, now.
5   Paul: ((walking back to the rock)) hm he's not being really
6   fair, is he?
7   John: (.) should we run away?
8   Paul: no, you do it. I'm gonna s- please,
9   I'll be your best friend. (.) run away. d- I'll wait
10   here. please, I'll let you be first. (.) kay.

In this excerpt, Paul proclaims that he found a bee and moves toward it (line 1). Rob opposes him, using aggravated commands ("do not step; get back on that rock, now"). The exaggerated stress on "step" and the temporal adverb "now" clearly state his opposition and imply threatening consequences if Paul does not comply. Paul states his opposition indirectly to John ("he's not being really fair, is he?", lines 5 and 6). He then begs John to defy Rob.

Excerpt 10 is a conflict where Paul proclaims he caught a bee (line 1), and Rob opposes him.

Excerpt (10)

1   Paul: I got one. ((going over to Rob and pointing
2   to something near him)) that- that kind.
3   Rob: Not a bee. Get back on the rock. Paul,
4   ( ) John, get down. got five times.
5   Rob: okay, Paul gets eleven times. Go, you can go
6   ( ). ((ushers John forward)) one,
7   Paul: ROB. ((John goes back to the rock,
8   and Paul takes a turn))
9   Rob: Six times. one, two, three, four, five. ((wanders
10   away))
11 Paul: John, point one out to me.
12 Rob: Get back on the rock. Paul, I counted to six.

Direct conflict strategies can be seen in Rob's use of an explicit polarity marker and aggravated command ("Not a bee; get back on the rock"), followed with physical gesture (ushering John over). In line 12, when Paul appears to delay beyond the allotted six-count, Rob opposes him with a direct command followed by one of his aggravated forms ("Get back on the rock. Paul, I counted to six").

In summary, when we compare the strategies of the two children who led the play in our two U.S. groups, Rob, the boy, was more direct in his strategies of stating and contesting opposition than the girl, Jenny. The boy used explicit markers of negative polarity and did not mitigate his opposition. He used aggravated, direct commands and verbs of telling, desire, and knowing. He used conditionals and adverbials to follow his oppositions with implied threat. In addition to these verbal strategies of conflict management that have been described previously in the literature for U.S. middle-class boys (Sheldon, 1990), Rob uses verbs of telling, desire, and knowing to aggravate commands and opposition. These data illustrate how more direct strategies are used in conflicts in U.S. middle-class boys' groups than in girls' groups.

Chinese Boys' Conflict Strategies in All-Boys Groups

The Chinese boys' conflict management strategies show a sharp contrast to those of the Chinese girls and U.S. boys. Censures and aggravated commands that are used by Chinese girls and U.S. boys were not deployed. Instead, Chinese boys use a combination of mitigated strategies, including mollification and justification (including warnings), as well as some unmitigated ones (including direct commands).

Conflicts in this same-sex triad involved Zhang and Gao siding against Li. In Excerpt 11, Li tries to preempt Gao's attempt to open the Play-Doh canister.

Excerpt (11): Children = Li (LI) = boy, Gao (GA) = boy, and Zhang (ZH) = boy

1 GA: ((tries hard to open Play-Doh box))
2 LI: ((walks to Gao's place)) wǒ lái nèng.
       I'll do it.
3 LI: ((Gao does not release)) Gao, wǒ lái bāng nǐ.
       Gao, I'm here to help you.
4 GA: ((tries to hold back, protesting))
5 GA: nǐ, wǒ nèng, wǒ gāngcái dǎkāi le.
       You, I do it. I just opened it. ((grabs canister))
6 LI: bié dòng.
       Don't move.
7 GA: āiya, wǒ dǎkāi le.
       Stop it. I've opened it.

8 LI: ((Gao refuses to give in)) dāihuǐr nǐ zài bǎ zhè
9   nèng huài le. lái, nǐ kàn. ((walks to own seat))
*   Later what if you break it? Come on, look.*

In line 2, Li initiates a conflict by using a proclamation ("I'll do it"). This move is preemptive because it intercepts what Gao is doing. Were Li to have stopped there, he would have approximated the American boys' conflict style. However, Li follows this direct request with a mollifying move in line 3. He presents his action as an offer of help ("Gao, I'm here to help you"). In so doing, the preemptive move is cast positively, mitigating the opposition. Mitigation is illustrated further by Gao in line 5, where he follows his counter challenge ("I do it") with a justification ("I just opened it"). In line 7, Gao follows a prohibitive refusal ("Stop it") with another justification ("I've just opened it"). Li opposes him by also using a justification ("Later, what if you break it"). This is in the form of a warning, which might be adultlike posturing.

Mollifying and mitigating strategies also can be seen in Excerpt 12.

Excerpt (12): LI = boy, ZH = boy, GA = boy

1 LI: ((sees a box on table, picks it up, says to Guo))
2   shūshu zhè xiǎohézi shì shénme ya?
    Uncle, what's this small box for?
3 ZH: ((moves to Li, going to help)) wǒ gěi nǐ dǎ kāi.
    I open it for you.
4 ZH: ((smells his own Play-Doh, says to self)) zhēn
5   xiāng.
    Smells so nice.
6 ZH: ((comes next to Li, stretches to grab Li's box)) wǒ
7   gěi nǐ dǎ kāi.
    I open it for you.
8 LI: ((hides box away from Zhang)) bù yòng, bù yòng.
    I don't need it. I don't need it.
9 GA: ((looks at Li opening box)) gēnběn nǐ dǎ bù kāi.
    You simply can't open it.
10 GA: nǐ bié dōu gěi shūshu sǎ méi,
    You'd better not to spill them on Uncle.
11 GA: bié gěi shūshu de nèng diū le,
    Better not to lose Uncle's stuff.
12 GA: bié gěi shūshu nèng diū le, shì ba! ((looks

13   at Zhang))
          Better not to lose Uncle's, right?

In lines 3 and 7, Zhang makes an offer to help Li open a box. Li refuses, using justification in line 8 ("I don't need it"). Notable are Gao's remarks in lines 9 to 11. Gao sides with Zhang but casts his opposition of Li in the form of justification ("You simply can't open it") and warning ("You'd better not spill them on Uncle. Better not lose Uncle's stuff").

Excerpts 11 and 12 suggest that Chinese boys' conflict management strategies are more similar to those of U.S. girls than to either Chinese girls or U.S. boys. Although they use direct strategies, including direct commands, they also use indirect ones, including mollification and reasoned argument.

Discussion of Conflict Strategies in Same-Sex Groups

In same-sex group interactions, the conflict strategies of the U.S. boys and Chinese girls are more direct than the strategies of U.S. girls and Chinese boys are. U.S. girls were the most mitigated in their strategies of expressing and contesting opposition. They used reframing of the play and mollification to avoid direct expression of conflict. Chinese girls were the most direct, using direct and third-party censures of copresent girls and rhetorical mocking questions, aggravated commands, and even threats and physical force. The American boys also used direct strategies. The boy who led the play in the episode used explicit markers of polarity, aggravated forms of commands, and implied threat. The other two boys seemed fearful and executed his bidding. The Chinese boys used a combination of direct and indirect strategies, starting out with forms that did not explicitly express disagreement and then resorting to direct commands, physical force, and put-downs. They also used reasoned argument. These conflict strategies were somewhat less assertive than those of Mandarin-speaking boys in Taiwan, who used aggravated commands and insistence rather than reasoned argument (Farris, 1999).

These findings are consistent with our survey of past research on children's conflict strategies, suggesting that gender differences in conflict strategies are culture specific. American middle-class girls in this study use mitigated strategies, similar to Sheldon's (1990, 1992, 1996) findings, whereas Chinese girls in this study use very direct strategies, similar to

Goodwin's (1990a, 1990b) finding concerning African American and Latina girls and Farris's (1991, 1999) findings concerning Mandarin-speaking girls in Taiwan. The findings in this study suggest that the SWH-suggested pattern of boys being more assertive than girls holds up for middle-class children in the United States but might be reversed in China.

Although it is difficult to pinpoint causes for cultural differences such as these, there are several possible contributing factors. One might be that certain contexts, such as discussion of moral norms, license females to be powerful in China but not in the United States. That females are licensed to be powerful in certain female-associated domains has been suggested for other cultures (see Cook-Gumperz & Szymanski, this issue, for a similar argument for Latino culture; see also Sherzer, 1987). Another possible contributing factor might be differences in the ways groups are formed and maintained in peer interactions. In the United States, as the research of Markus and Kitayama (1991) suggests, groups might be more fleeting and need greater interactive maintenance work. Because conflict plays an important role in the maintenance of group boundaries (Coser, 1954, 1967), Americans might have to worry about interactions that threaten the group. Indeed, Corsaro (1985) found that American children have to work hard to gain access to and maintain groups. Hence, American girls might have to be wary of overt conflict. The strong hierarchical structure that we observed in the American boys' group also might result from the fleetingness of groups in this culture. A strong leader might be needed because without strong leadership, the group might not hold together.

In contrast, in China, where "interdependent construal of the self" (Markus & Kitayama, 1991) is culturally valued, groups are taken for granted and members of a peer group might not have to strive as hard to maintain group boundaries. One ramification of such taken-for-granted group structure might be that children do not have to work hard to maintain group boundaries. Chinese girls therefore can afford to use direct and aggravated conflict strategies, and Chinese boys do not need a hierarchical group structure, resulting in their use of the more mitigated conflict strategies. These conclusions are highly tentative, but many such factors might contribute to the cultural differences observed in this study.

According to the SWH, girls' more mitigated strategies developed in their same-sex group interactions will put them at a disadvantage in mixed-sex interactions where boys use aggravated strategies (Coates, 1986). Given the greater directness of the Chinese girls' strategies of conflict management observed here when compared to the American girls, and the greater indirectness of the Chinese boys when compared to the American boys, what are the implications for cross-sex conflict? Are American girls more disadvantaged in cross-sex conflict than Chinese girls?

American Girls' and Boys' Conflict Strategies in Mixed-Sex Groups

The U.S. cross-sex friendship group that we observed sometimes instantiated courtship-like scenarios. In these scenarios, the boys courted Jenny's favor (e.g., "Jenny can you please make me a heart?") and Jenny sometimes gained magical powers. She was positioned as powerful in these scenarios, which can be described as "borderwork," play that emphasizes gender boundaries, such as girls and boys taking sides against each other in games or chasing one another (Thorne, 1993). Example 13 is an example of conflict in this group.

Excerpt (13) Children = Rob, Jenny (Dawn)

```
 1  Jenny:  guys look. doggie, come here. look doggie.
 2          doggie, look.
 3  Rob:    what is it?
 4  Jenny:  I don't know.
 5  Rob:    it's magic. it's magic. an alien ( ) I feel
 6          something ((starts growling and shaking))
 7  Jenny:  I feel something too ((shaking))
 8  Rob:    no. it doesn't happen to you.
 9  Jenny:  I feel ⌈something too?⌉
10  Rob:          ⌊it only    ⌋ happens to dogs, please? Jenny,
11          can you only have it happen to dogs?
12  Jenny:  no 'cause I found this first.
13  Rob:    please? I'll do anything you say. please?
14          please, Jenny? please?
15  Jenny:  but this makes everybody feel funny.
16  Rob:    no. it doesn't make you feel funny. you're the
17          one with the magic, please?
18  Jenny:  well. I kinda said that I wanted to ( ) didn't I?
19          ( ) I feel something in my head.
20  Rob:    can we both go down and die?
```

In this excerpt, Jenny and Rob are in the yard, and Jenny has magical powers that have turned Rob into her "doggie." They break out of character at one point to dispute the rules of the game. Here, Rob uses mitigated forms. He pleads with Jenny (e.g., "[it only] happens to dogs, please? Jenny, can you only have it happen to dogs?", lines 10 and 11).

Jenny seems to be dominant in this scenario and wins the dispute over whether the magic can affect her. She uses more assertive strategies than she used in her all-girl friendship group. In line 12, she uses a negative polarity marker ("No, 'cause I found this first"). In line 18, she uses an aggravated command with a verb of saying ("I kinda said that I wanted too, didn't I?").

Rob's strategies are more mitigated than those that he used in his same-sex friendship. Although he still uses negative polarity markers, he asks permission ("please? Jenny, can you only have it happen to dogs?"), pleads ("Please, Jenny, please?"), and bargains ("Please, I'll do anything you say"). We never saw him pleading, trying to compromise, or asking permission in his same-sex group. Jenny wins the dispute in the end. In line 20, the resolution of the conflict, stated with Rob's permission request ("Can we both go down and die?") is that she will be affected by the magic and will lie down and die. The magic will not, as Rob wishes, "happen only to dogs."

In these American children's play, girls appeared highly positioned in courtship-like scenarios. This is consistent with past research suggesting that women's power might be restricted to specific spheres of influence (Sherzer, 1987), and the previous data suggest that courtship might be one such sphere for American girls and women. Contradicting the predictions of the SWH, girls used more assertive strategies than in their same-sex groups and often dominated boys.

However, in other scenarios we observed, American girls were positioned as subordinate. Excerpt 14 depicts a scenario describable as doctor play, which is about work outside the home.

Excerpt (14) Children = Jenny, Rob, Peg   Spring

```
1  Peg:    hey. you wanna play (.) doc::tor=?
2  Jenny:  =YOU'RE (DO ⌈(    )⌉)
3  Rob:               ⌊ yeah.⌋ I'm the doctor.
4  Peg:    (.) okay. (.) you're the doctor. but I havta lie
5          on the counter ((climbing back up on the bench))
```

```
 6              ┌( )┐?
 7   Rob:       └you┘'re the nurse. ((waving his hand at Jenny))
 8   Jenny:    (.) yeah.
 9   Rob:      ((reaching over and turning tape recorder off))
10              (.) but. ┌turn      ┐ this off.
11   Jenny:             └(and we-)┘ ((Peg gets off the bench
12              and walks away)) (.) yeah. and I'm checking
13              what- (.) what- how- how- how si::ck she is.
14              ((turning the pages of her book))
15   Rob:       ┌.. no::. (.) let me:: che::ck.] ((sitting down
16              └next to Jenny and looking straight at her))
17   Jenny:    [.. no. (.) I'm supposed to check.]= ((looking at
18              Rob))
19   Rob:      =nunh-unh.
20   Jenny:    (.) uhuh.
21   Rob:      =do::ctors are.
22   Jenny:    =cau- NO::.
23   Rob:      =NO::. NURSES just loo::k.
24   Jenny:    (.) unh-unh.
```

In this excerpt, Rob relegates Jenny, who wants to be the doctor, to the role of a nurse (line 7). He uses more assertive strategies of managing conflict than he used in Excerpt 13. Assertive conflict strategies can be seen in the use of negative polarity markers and direct commands ("No, let me check," line 15), insistence ("Nunh-unh," line 19), and imperatives ("doctors are" and "NURSES just look," lines 21 and 23).

Although Jenny uses more direct conflict strategies than in her same-sex group, she does not get what she wants. She uses a negative polarity marker followed by an imperative ("No, I'm supposed to check"). She also uses insistence in line 20 ("uhuh"). In line 22, she uses the negative polarity marker "NO," stated loudly. Despite these direct tactics, she is interrupted by Rob in line 23 ("NO, NURSES just look") and loses the dispute. Jenny does not get to examine the patient.

These data indicate that in American children's play, girls appear more highly positioned in courtship-like scenarios than in other scenarios. The dominance was not predictable from patterns of language expression observed in the same-sex groups, and there was contextual variation in it.

Chinese Girls' and Boys' Conflict Strategies in Mixed-Sex Groups

In the Chinese mixed-sex group we observed, there was also contextual complexity in the effectiveness of conflict strategies. Conflicts usually involved the two girls, Fu and Sun, siding against the boy, Li. These disputes occurred when Li appropriated goods or showed off. The girls opposed Li by attacking his moral character, meanness, cheek, inappropriateness, or craziness. Excerpt 15 is a conflict in which Li does not let Fu use the knife.

Excerpt (15): LI = boy, FU = girl, SU = girl

1 LI: ((takes a toy knife from in front of Fu's table))
2 LI: zhè shì wǒ de dāodao.
3   *This is my knife.*
4 FU: zhēn shì de, duì ba? [zhēn jiāoqì].
        That's mean, isn't it? Really fussy. ((to Sun))
5 SU: ((gives own knife to Fu)) [en. gěi nǐ, gěi nǐ.]
        Mmm. Here is one. Here is one.
6 FU: (putting Play-Doh into boxes, to Sun)) bù yòng.
        That's OK.
7 SU: ((to Li)) zhè yòu bù shì nǐmen jiā de
8   *This even doesn't belong to your house.*
9 SU: nǐ yòu bù ná huí jiā.
        It's not that you will take it home.
10 FU: ((giggles))
11 SU: shuō nǐ de dāozi?
        And you (have the cheek to) say it is your knife?
12 SU: běnlái jiù bù ná huí jiā,
        It's out of the question that you will take it home.
13 SU: duì ba, shūshu, shì bù shì?
        Isn't that right, uncle? Isn't it?

In response to Li's stating "This is my knife" in line 2, the girls use a medley of assertive strategies. Fu counters with a third-party complaint to Sun, stating "That's mean, isn't it? Really fussy." In line 7, Sun elaborates on Fu's censure with a direct criticism "This even doesn't belong to your house," and in line 11, Sun censures him further, using a rhetorical question ("And you have the cheek to say it is your knife?"), although Li has said nothing. This is followed by a form as aggravated as any we observed the American boys using in their same-sex conflicts. In line 12, Sun states, "It's out of the question that you will take it home." The girls use the same direct strategies they used in their same-sex group, including direct and third-party censures, rhetorical questions, and aggravated commands. Later in the play session, the two girls resume third-party complaints about Li's knife transgression ("Li is really fussy, isn't he?"), and Li finally concedes the dispute ("I let you use it now, is it okay?"). That these Chinese girls could dominate cross-sex conflicts goes against a literalist interpretation of the SWH, although it is consistent with their language expression in the same-sex group.

Despite their use of assertive strategies, there were surprising moments in this cross-sex interaction where the girls deferred to Li. This is illustrated in Excerpt 16.

Excerpt (16): LI = boy, SU = girl, FU = girl

1 LI: ((presses; Play-Doh strips emerge from pressor))
2 SU: ha, ha, ha, ha
3 FU: ((watching Li, says to Sun)) piàoliàng de, duì ba?
      beautiful ones, right?
4 SU: ((watching Li)) ei you, zhēn piàoliàng ei.
      wow, really gorgeous.
5 FU: ((watching as Li's Play-Doh runs out)) méi le.
      It's all gone.
6 LI: wǒ nòng de piào bù piàoliàng?
      Is what I made beautiful or not?
7 FU: piàoliàng.
      beautiful.
8 SU: (giggling) jiù gēn nà dà shǐkèlàngzi shì de.
      just like the shit-eating bugs.
9 FU: (giggles then stops) bié shuō nàme ěxīn de huà
      don't say things that gross.

In this episode, the girls are an audience to Li's technical skill. In line 3, Fu says Li's product is beautiful, and then Sun agrees in line 4 that it is "really gorgeous." Although later in the excerpt, Sun contradicts this admiration with one of her usually assertive, mocking statements in line 8 ("Just like the shit-eating bugs"), this session does not escalate into conflict (thanks to Fu's comment in line 9), and the positive regard of Li's product is allowed to stand. This is in marked contrast to some of the other examples, where the girls mocked Li's products (e.g., "It's a little yellow") or ability ("Are you a little crazy") when he tried to show off. In technical matters, when it did not get in the way of goods they wanted to access, these girls, despite the assertive strategies in their repertoire, sometimes gave the boy the upper hand.

Both the Chinese and U.S. data from cross-sex conflict suggest contextual complexity in the use of conflict strategies. Children can use strategies other than those learned or practiced in their same-sex groups. Moreover, despite the strategy, selected outcomes can depend on positioning by others (e.g., Jenny uses assertive conflict strategies in both Excerpts 13 and 14 but wins only in the former).

CONCLUSIONS

The data presented in this study suggest that there are both cultural and contextual differences in how gender is indexed through talk (Ochs, 1992; West & Zimmerman, 1987). From the conflict strategies used in same-sex talk, assertiveness is a more valued stance for Chinese middle-class girls than it is for U.S. middle-class girls. In contrast, assertiveness is less emphasized as a valued stance for Chinese middle-class boys than it is for U.S. middle-class boys. Our results concerning Chinese girls are similar to those of studies that examined African American and Latino children's conflict styles (Goodwin, 1990a, 1990b, 1995). Unlike their American middle-class counterparts, girls in these cultures do not appear to be under a constraint to be nice or sensitive, or to "say it with a smile" (Sachs, 1987, p. 188).

These comparative differences in children's talk might stem from the adult cultures. There are valued stances for women and men that are domain specific (Sherzer, 1987) as well as culture specific. In China, as argued by Farris (in press), the culture's dualism positions women in two roles, the silent wife and the good mother. In the latter role, women are positioned as strong, authoritative figures. In contrast, past sociolinguistic studies indicate a quite different positioning of women in U.S. middle-class families. Request forms received from the children and participation frameworks in dinner-time narratives indicate that American middle-class women are not positioned powerfully within the family (Ervin-Tripp, O'Connor, & Rosenberg, 1984; Ochs, 1992; Ochs & Taylor, 1992). These roles of adult women are mirrored in children's play. In talk among girls, where family scenes are enacted, we see Chinese girls using assertive strategies, whereas American girls use mitigated strategies.

Another possible explanation of the cultural differences might come from group theory. Conflict has an important role in the negotiation of group boundaries (Coser, 1954, 1967). In Chinese culture, which values an interdependent construal of the self (Markus & Kitayama, 1991), the group is presupposed and exaggerated efforts are not needed to hold the group together. Hence, in China, we observe less direct boys' conflict strategies and more direct girls' conflict strategies.

The SWH claims that gendered communicative strategies are consistent across contexts. Accordingly, one might assume from the expression that occurred in same-sex groups that Chinese girls would be advantaged in cross-sex conflict. However, what happens in the mixed-sex group interactions is not easily predictable from same-sex group interactions. Chinese girls have very assertive conflict strategies in their repertoire but are not always positioned as dominant. Neither are American girls, who use mitigated strategies in same-sex interactions, always disadvantaged when interacting with boys.

The findings suggest contextual complexity in the consequences of conflict strategies. The dominance depends not on sociolinguistic competence alone, but also on a number of contextual factors. The gender constitution of the group and the girl–boy ratio no doubt are important. The outnumbering of boys by girls in the mixed-sex triad of Chinese children is likely to have influenced the girls' dominance. The theme of the activity plays an important role, as children index models of complementary gender relations in their talk (Cameron, 1996) that appear to depend on context. An American boy might willingly take a subordinate role to a girl in a courtship-like scenario but not in a scenario about work. Chinese girls might concede to boys in technical matters under some circumstances but not others. These displays of complementary gender relations reflect a constructive role in children's production of gender. Moreover, children can choose not to go along with the models of gender relations indexed by others, as when Jenny resisted the less powerful role of a nurse by using assertive conflict strategies. In that children instantiate different models of complementary gender relations at different moments of cross-sex play, their constructions of gender are not fixed reproductions of the adult culture. Children's uses of gender show a "fluctuating significance . . . in the ongoing scenes of social life" (Thorne, 1993, p. 61).

The findings from this study, then, suggest that children have an active, productive role in the construction of gender. The children incorporate models of gender relations from the adult culture, as seen in the comparative differences between Chinese and American children, but they also instantiate these models in different ways in different contexts. The SWH, although attributing a constructive role to children's articulation of gender, emphasizes neither the cultural character nor the contextual fluidity of this articulation.

REFERENCES

Bing, J. M., & Bergvall, V. L. (1996). The question of questions: Beyond binary thinking. In V. L. Bergvall, J. M. Bing, & A. F. Freed (Ed.), *Rethinking language and gender research: Theory and practice* (pp. 1–30). London: Longman.

Cameron, D. (1996). The language–gender interface: Challenging co-optation. In V. L. Bergvall, J. M. Bing, & A. F. Freed (Eds.), *Rethinking language and gender research: Theory and practice* (pp. 31–53). London: Longman.

Coates, J. (1986). *Women, men, and language.* London: Longman.

Corsaro, W. A. (1985). *Friendship and peer culture in the early years.* Norwood, NJ: Ablex.

Coser, L. A. (1954). *The functions of social conflict.* Glencoe, IL: Free Press.

Coser, L. A. (1967). *Continuities in the study of social conflict.* New York: Free Press.

Ervin-Tripp, S. M., & Gordon, D. (1984). The structure of children's requests. In R. L. Schiefelbush & J. Pickar (Eds.), *The acquisition of communicative competence* (pp. 298–321). Baltimore: University Park Press.

Ervin-Tripp, S. M., O'Connor, M. C., & Rosenberg, J. (1984). Language and power in the family. In M. Shultz & C. Kramarae (Eds.), *Language and power* (pp. 116–135). Belmont, CA: Sage.

Farris, C. S. (1991). The gender of child discourse: Same-sex peer socialization through language use in a Taiwanese preschool. *Journal of Linguistic Anthropology, 2,* 198–224.

Farris, C. S. (1999). *Cross-sex peer conflict and the discursive production of gender in a Chinese preschool in Taiwan.* Manuscript submitted for publication.

Farris, C. S. (in press). Silence and speaking: Preschool students in Taiwan discursively produce Chinese gendered subjectivities. *Anthropology and Education Quarterly.*

Goodwin, M. H. (1990a). *He-said-she-said: Talk as social organization among Black children.* Bloomington: Indiana University Press.

Goodwin, M. H. (1990b). Tactical uses of stories: Participation frameworks within girls' and boys' disputes. *Discourse Processes, 13,* 33–71.

Goodwin, M. H. (1995). Co-construction in girls' hopscotch. *Research on Language and Social Interaction, 28,* 261–282.

Goodwin, M. H. (1998). Games of stance: Conflict and footing in hopscotch. In S. Hoyle & C. T. Adger (Eds.), *Kids talk: Language practices of older children* (pp. 23–46). New York: Oxford University Press.

Guo, J. (1999, May). *Culture and context in gender differences in communicative strategies: Perspectives from U.S. and Chinese children.* Presentation given at the Department Colloquium of the Psychology Department, Chinese University of Hong Kong.

Kyratzis, A. (in press). Constituting the emotions: A longitudinal study of emotion talk in a preschool friendship group of boys. In H. Kotthoff & B. Baron (Eds.), *Gender in interaction.* Amsterdam: Benjamins.

Kyratzis, A., & Guo, J. (1996). "Separate worlds" for girls and boys?: Views from U.S. and Chinese mixed-sex friendship groups. In D. I. Slobin, J. Gerhardt, A. Kyratzis, & J. Guo (Eds.), *Social interaction, social context, and language: Essays in honor of Susan Ervin-Tripp* (pp. 555–578). Mahwah, NJ: Lawrence Erlbaum Associates, Inc.

Maltz, D. N., & Borker, R. A. (1982). A cultural approach to male–female miscommunication. In J. J. Gumperz (Ed.), *Communication, language and social identity* (pp. 196–216). Cambridge, England: Cambridge University Press.

Markus, H. R., & Kitayama, S. (1991). Culture and the self: Implications for cognition, emotion, and motivation. *Psychological Review, 98,* 224–253.

Ochs, E. (1992). Indexing gender. In A. Duranti & C. Goodwin (Eds.), *Rethinking context: Language as an interactive phenomenon. Studies in the social and cultural foundations of language, 11* (pp. 335–358). Cambridge, England: Cambridge University Press.

Ochs, E., & Taylor, C. (1992). Mothers' role in the everyday reconstruction of "Father knows best." In K. Hall, M. Bucholtz, & B. Moonwomon (Eds.), *Locating power: Proceedings of the second Berkeley Women and Language Conference* (pp. 447–462). Berkeley, CA: Berkeley Women and Language Group.

Sachs, J. (1987). Preschool girls' and boys' language use in pretend play. In S. U. Phillips, S. Steele, & C. Tanz (Eds.), *Language, gender, and sex in comparative perspective* (pp. 178–188). Cambridge, England: Cambridge University Press.

Sheldon, A. (1990). Pickle fights: Gendered talk in preschool disputes. *Discourse Processes, 13,* 5–31.

Sheldon, A. (1992). Conflict talk: Sociolinguistic challenges to self-assertion and how young girls meet them. *Merrill-Palmer Quarterly, 38,* 95–117.

Sheldon, A. (1996). You can be the baby brother but you aren't born yet: Preschool girls' negotiation for power and access in pretend play. *Research on Language and Social Interaction, 29,* 57–80.

Sherzer, J. (1987). A diversity of voices: Men's and women's speech in ethnographic perspective. In S. U. Phillips, S. Steele, & C. Tanz (Eds.), *Language, gender, and sex in comparative perspective* (pp. 95–119). Cambridge, England: Cambridge University Press.

Tannen, D. (1990). *You just don't understand: Women and men in conversation.* New York: Ballantine Books.

Thorne, B. (1993). *Gender play: Girls and boys in school.* New Brunswick, NJ: Rutgers University Press.

West, C., & Zimmerman, D. H. (1987). Doing gender. *Gender & Society, 1,* 125–151.

Research on Language and Social Interaction, 34(1), 75–106

Organizing Participation in Cross-Sex Jump Rope: Situating Gender Differences Within Longitudinal Studies of Activities

Marjorie Harness Goodwin
Department of Anthropology
University of California, Los Angeles

This study investigates how children use directives and forms of exclusion to organize play activity. Elementary school children of mixed ethnicity were observed playing the game of jump rope over the span of 1 month. Girls' dominance in the game was observed to change over time. In mixed-sex groups where boys were learning how to jump, girls frequently set the agenda regarding how the game was to be played. However, as boys gained proficiency in the game, they became equal partners in calling plays and making decisions. Rather than finding differences in directive forms related to gender, I find that the ability to use actions that tell others what to do in a very direct fashion in cross-sex interaction changes over time, as children become more skilled in the activity. Ethnographically based studies are essential to examine how the social orchestration of an activity can change over time.

The separate worlds hypothesis (SWH) states that "boys and girls come from different sociolinguistic subcultures, having learned to do different things with words in a conversation" (Maltz & Borker, 1982, p. 200). Girls use language to create and maintain relationships of closeness and equality; their "play is cooperative and activities are usually organized in noncompetitive ways" (p. 205), contrasting with boys' hierarchical

---

Correspondence concerning this article should be sent to Marjorie Harness Goodwin, Department of Anthropology, University of California, Los Angeles, CA 90095. E-mail: mgoodwin@anthro.ucla.edu

forms of social organization. Arguing from ethnographic work in the Middle East and southern Europe, where extreme gender segregation exists,[1] Maltz and Borker stated that physical separation and involvement in different types of activities leads to "sexually differentiated communicative cultures" (p. 200), which result in miscommunication between boys and girls.[2]

Recent work has attempted to avoid dichotomies that essentialize sex–gender differences. Ethnographic research on the conversational practices of a working-class African American children's neighborhood peer group (Goodwin, 1980), for example, finds that boys and girls (ages 4–13) frequently are in one another's copresence and make use of many of the same argument strategies in cross-sex interaction; moreover, girls hold their own in cross-sex disputes and can top their male counterparts. Although themes of girls as cooperative and boys as conflictual are found in much of the social science research on sex–gender differences (Adler, Kless, & Adler, 1992; Leaper, 1991; Maccoby, 1990; Miller, Danaher, & Forbes, 1986; Sachs, 1987),[3] researchers such as Goodwin (1990, 1998) and Sheldon (1992, 1996) have demonstrated that girls as well as boys can engage in highly assertive exchanges. Sheldon found that girls' assertiveness frequently was masked. In her studies of the conflict talk of educationally and socially advantaged middle-class American urban preschool children engaging in pretend play, Sheldon (1996) found that girls use "double-voice discourse"—a style that permits speakers to "confront without being very confrontational; to clarify without backing down; and to use mitigators, indirectness, and even subterfuge to soften the blow while promoting their own wishes" (p. 61). Goodwin (1980, 1990) found that African American working-class urban girls (ages 7–12) in their neighborhood engage in highly public disputes called "he said she said." Power in the girls' peer group results from being able to orchestrate elaborate realignments of the social order through storytelling. Girls frame their accusations against girls they accuse of having talked about them behind their backs as reports learned about through a third party: "Kerry said you said I said X." Because the intermediate party rather than the current speaker is credited with authorship of the report of the offense, the defendant cannot bring a counter accusation against her accuser in the immediate encounter, and disputes are not resolved easily. Dispute processes can endure for weeks. Ostracism can result; periods of ridicule and insulting siblings and parents of the targeted girl stemming from disputes can become so intense that families consider leaving the neighborhood.

Kyratzis and Guo (1996) noted that there has been relatively little research examining the reality of children's separate worlds cross-cultur-ally. Studying American and Mainland Chinese preschoolers in mixed-sex interactions, they found that although American boys used more direct unmitigated forms than girls, Chinese girls used more aggravated direc-tives, ratified by boys' compliance, within pretend play. In a study of pre-school children in urban Taiwan, Farris (2000) found girls made use of a direct, confrontational style. Goodwin's (1994, 1998) work looking at interaction among bilingual Spanish–English-speaking, working-class, second- through fifth-grade girls playing hopscotch challenges stereotyp-ical notions of girls' cooperative language styles.

This study investigates the use of directives and forms of exclusion among fourth-grade children in mixed-sex groups in an ethnically mixed elementary school in southern California. In previous work (Goodwin 1980, 1990), I found differences in how girls and boys organized task activities, with boys using more aggravated forms that differentiated speakers from recipients. In the midst of a different context—games—analyzed here, I find that the ability to use actions that tell others what to do in a very direct fashion in cross-sex interaction changes over time, as members of a same-sex playgroup become more skilled in the perform-ance of the activity. Both girls and boys in positions of power use direct forms to organize the activity and exclude children.

THE GROUP AND FIELD SETTING

The study, based on 6 months of fieldwork during 1997, examines directive use within a common cultural activity system: the game of jump rope.[4] It was conducted in collaboration with Jill Kushner, Sarah Meacham, and Fazila Bhimji, who assisted in videotaping over 60 hr of interaction. The elementary school, called Hanley, draws children from various parts of the city, although the children studied here are primarily middle class. In many public schools of Los Angeles, the space where children eat lunch and play is highly circumscribed; children even might have to walk silently in single file from one confined area to another. However, at Hanley, during their lunch break, children are free to eat and move about across various spaces with whomever they choose on either of two rather expansive playgrounds, with many shady areas affording alternative types of spaces and activities.[5] Girls and boys ate lunch separately on picnic tables, which were located close enough for children to yell back and forth to one another.

During recess, where girls and boys participate in a number of activities in their same-sex groups, they are not separated physically. The model "with then apart," described by Thorne (1993), characterizes much of children's play. Fourth through sixth graders had lunch and recess period at the same time. Two sixth-grade girls who were athletes regularly organized basketball games with boys; generally, however, games such as basketball, softball, soccer, or football were played only occasionally by girls. Girls did not enjoy playing with boys, because they felt they played aggressively and only occasionally passed the ball to girls. Boys wolfed down their lunches as rapidly as possible so that they could get balls from an equipment shed and lay claim to the playing field. Until "fair school" policies were implemented, putting into place a rotating schedule for soccer and football including girls as well as boys, one male college student playground assistant supported the boys' claim that the playing field was rightfully a boys' rather than a girls' space.

Fourth-grade boys alternated between basketball, soccer, volleyball, roaming the schoolyard and causing mischief (locking people in the equipment shed), talking with girls, and jumping rope.[6] Several groups of girls with different orientations toward play were evident in the schoolyard. In 1997, although third-grade boys and girls played handball and basketball together quite frequently, fourth-grade boys and girls only rarely participated in these games together. A group of fourth- through sixth-grade girls who were bilingual English–Spanish speakers participated in jump rope, joke telling, or swinging on tires with a bilingual boy. Other fourth-grade girls sat on the swings or jungle gyms and talked among themselves and with boys.

Occasionally, girls played volleyball with boys. The particular group of fourth-grade girls whose interaction is examined in this study preferred the activities of talking and playing jump rope together in their same-sex group. The girls' group in this report included two Japanese American girls, an African American girl, two White girls, and a South Asian girl. The boys' group included an African American, a Mexican American, a Japanese American, and five Whites.

Although frequently regarded as a girls' game, during May and June 1997, jump rope at Hanley was an activity that was promoted by the coaches and played during physical education classes by both boys and girls.[7] Both groups played three variations on the game. The most common way the game was played involved jumping to a rhyme, such as Teddy Bear, Texaco Mexico, Ice Cream Soda, or Cinderella. In another game called "clock," children lined up behind each other; each player in turn would jump into the moving rope and jump progressively higher numbers of jumps (1–12). A third version of the game was "speed jumping": jumping as the rope was turned at a very fast pace. The boys' favorite version of speed jumping involved multiple children jumping inside the rope simultaneously; when someone missed, he was eliminated from the rope. Each time they jumped, they would try to beat their own former record. Although generally girls jumped with members of their own clique, one recess period fourth-grade girls challenged fifth-grade girls to a contest to see who could jump rope to 100 first.

Because jump rope was played with enthusiasm by both girls and boys, it provides an unusual context for analyzing how different gender groups organize the activity and make use of directives in same- and cross-sex interaction. Although it is commonly considered a game lacking in complexity (Borman, 1982; Borman & Frankel, 1984; Lever, 1976; Piaget, 1932/1965), in fact a great deal of negotiation occurs regarding every aspect of the game. Movements requiring athletic agility take place in the midst of some of the rhymes of jump rope. In the game entitled Texaco Mexico,[8] players must jump in the air while doing kicks, splits, turning around, touching the ground, "paying their taxes" (by slapping the hand of a turner), and "getting outta town" (jumping out of the rope) while the rope is in motion.

REGULATING ACTIVITY THROUGH DIRECTIVES

Directives, actions that are designed to get someone else to do something, are used to make bids regarding how the activity should proceed. The grammatical shape of directives varies during different phases of the activity. In keeping with Ervin-Tripp's (1976) perspective, it is important to note that directive forms in no way "lie along a scale of increasing politeness for all social conditions" (p. 60). Bald imperatives such as "Faster. Come on!", "Not too early!", "Okay. Turn it!", or "Get in more!" help regulate the activity. They are the expected or unmarked types of actions in the midst of the activity of rope, as they promote the game's onward development or critique the style in which it is being played

(Goodwin, 1990). As Brown and Levinson (1978) and Bellinger and Gleason (1982) argued, the situation of the moment itself might warrant the use
of a directive format that in other circumstances would be seen as aggravated. At junctures in play activity, however, directives might take a more
indirect form (Goodwin, 1990, pp. 316–317); rather than making demands,
children make proposals about possible courses of action using "Let's" as
in "Let's see how many people can get in at one time" (said by a boy during same-sex play) or "Let's play a game snake" (a girl's utterance).

Labov and Fanshell (1977) argued that "in all discussions of discourse, analysts take into account the subject's desire to mitigate or mod-
ify his expression to avoid creating offense" (p. 84). Some directive
formats suggest that the addressee has complete control over whether the
requested action in fact will be performed (e.g., "Can I turn the rope?").
As Gordon and Ervin-Tripp (1984) argued, such "conventional polite
requests, with few exceptions, are interrogatives that appear to offer the
hearer options in responding. . . . Conventional polite forms . . . avoid the
appearance of trying to control or impose on another" (p. 308). Alternative to such "mitigated" types of requests, directives might be formulated
in a more aggravated fashion, becoming more demanding while increasing directness (Eisenberg & Garvey, 1981)—as in imperatives ("Give me
the rope!"). The embodied ways in which directives are formulated and
responded to can create contrastive forms of social organization (Goodwin, 1990). Although many studies of directives ignore responses of recipients, ethologically oriented researchers of children's dominance
hierarchies have argued that a crucial feature of social conflict is its interactional nature, which "requires that equal attention be given to the activity of both participants in the aggressive social exchange" (Strayer &
Strayer, 1980, p. 154). Directives and responses to them affirm and ratify
who has the right to make decisions about various optional ways that the
game can be played. They are especially powerful types of moves in deciding the scope of participation in the game.

Although the children enjoyed playing with their friends in groups of
four to six or more, the larger the size of the group, the more time it took
for someone to get their next turn at jumping. Children attempted to
exclude children who were not core members of their friendship group.
Boys had more inclusive groups than girls but limited the participation of
those who did not have the same skills as the other members of the playgroup—for example, by making them turners. Thus, a critical site for the
examination of directive use is in decision making about roles in the game

and the organization of jump rope. In this article, I explore the accomplishment of such tasks in mixed-sex groups where first girls and later boys are dominant. An important dimension of this study is that it investigates changing social roles for defining rules over time; as children become more skilled in the activity, the forms of speech actions they invoke to construct social identities shift as well. Two jump rope sessions held 1 month apart are investigated with respect to how directives are used and provide alternative forms of participation frameworks. First, however, I briefly sketch how the game is played in same-sex groups.

BOYS' SAME-SEX JUMP ROPE

Different types of social orders are constructed by boys in the midst of jump rope. Analyzing a particular session of jump rope (held May 12, 1997) among members of a group that included six White boys and one Japanese American boy, Wingard (1998) found that a hierarchical structure emerged in which a particular boy's directives were treated as binding, whereas others' were not. One boy had the power to orchestrate participation in the activity, whereas others exercised relatively little control over their own participation. In the boys' group, Malcolm was the leader. His abilities to jump rope were superior to the other boys; he could jump continuously for longer periods of time than any other boy. His superior jumping skill led to his authority to control the activity with respect to (a) commenting on the players' performances ("Everyone's messing up!") and (b) determining who could take which roles in the activity— who could play and turn the rope. Malcolm denied the opportunity to turn the rope to a particular player the group wanted to exclude in utterances such as "NO:: TOM! Tom you can't do it!" *((grabbing the rope from Tom and pushing him out of the way))*

Malcolm delivered directives in the imperative form: "Make it touch the ground! And turn it right!" or "Slow it down Tom!" It was his directives regarding who should turn the rope, what the speed of the rope should be, or who could take the next turn at jumping that are ratified by others in the group; generally, his directives were accepted with minimal contestation. In fact, other boys frequently echoed the directives he gave as they attempt to affiliate with him.

Tom, the least coordinated boy of the group, had great difficulty jumping over the rope and initially was denied his request to participate as a turner. Eventually, he got to play when Malcolm overturned the other boys' mandate that Tom not be permitted to participate. As Tom ran to pick up the rope when someone dropped it, Malcolm stated, "Let Tom DO it." Malcolm changed participant roles at his own whim. He later reversed the group's characterization of Tom as a bad turner and defended him. When a boy said, "Tom's doing it way up here" *((holding rope high))*, Malcolm responded, "Watch. Tom's doing it right. Look. See. Tom's doing it right."

Whereas Malcolm's directives were formulated as imperatives, Tom's directives took the form of statements of future action such as "I'll turn." Tom offered to take the ends of the rope rather than demanding that others give it to him. His relative powerlessness was evident in the fact that in 9 out of 10 attempts, the boys refused to give him the ends of the rope. Thus, although Malcolm's directives were either ratified or echoed by other boys, Tom's requests received no uptake and in fact were refuted. The boys also felt at liberty to critique his turning style. Dramatic differences in power thus were made evident through interaction in directive–response sequences.

A quite different type of arrangement occurred 3 days later on May 15, 1997. Rather than refusing Tom a role, Fred aligned with him through several moves: (a) He was coached in his jumping ("Tom you're jumping too late"); (b) he was given a second chance when he failed ("You can go again"); and (c) he was offered the role of turner ("Let's let Tom be an all time turner!"). In a form of "twinning ritual," Fred said that Tom's jumping was similar to his own: "I'm jumping too early too. Tom, I don't blame you." When Tom said "I'd rather spin than jump," Fred replied, "That's like me Tom." Rather than excluding Tom, he was given a role and told that his performance in the game is no different from one of the other principal players. Boys thus can create exclusive or inclusive types of social arrangements through language.

GIRLS' SAME-SEX JUMP ROPE

Within the girls' group, no clear leader emerged to control the activity in the six-girl clique. Jumping ability did not determine status or roles in the activity. Although Janis was the worst jumper in the group (the reason for her exclusion in a cross-sex jump rope contest, in example 22), in same-sex play she was as assertive as any other player in the game and assumed the role of spokesperson for the group when boys were onlookers (See examples 2–4, 6–7). Janis and Emi were considered the trendsetters for the group, and their opinions were more respected than those of other group members. (See Emi's directives in examples 2, 6, 26, and 28.) Dispute among members of the girls' group was quite common and not restricted to particular girls. In the girls' group, power to orchestrate the activity (naming the rhyme that would be chanted, deciding who played what roles, determining how many jumps were permitted before someone forfeited a turn, etc.) or challenge turners' style of moving the rope or a jumper's moves was distributed more equally among group members than in the boys' group. (Example 10 shows four of the five girls calling out rules in cross-sex interaction.) By way of example, the following shows the way multiple players rather than one party designating herself as leader dispute a jumper's complaint about the way the rope is being turned:

Example 1 4/4/97 12:59:00

Sarah:	Guys you're going too slow!
	((hands extended))
Lonnie:	⌈ Sarah it's not their fault!
Emi:	⌊ No they aren't Sarah.
	⌈ It's ( )
Sarah:	⌊ Well to <u>me</u> it's slow!
Kesha:	Then say <u>fa</u>ster Sarah.
Lonnie:	When you're <u>jump</u> roping
	you say faster.
Sarah:	O<u>kay</u>. Just turn.

Although ability to direct, critique, and counter was not restricted to particular individuals in the girls' group (as in many sessions of boys' jump rope), forms of exclusion occurred more frequently, across a range of activities. One girl, a working-class girl who was older and more phys-ically mature than the other girls, was called a "tag-along" by herself and members of the clique; she attempted to play with the group despite the fact that she was ridiculed frequently and ostracized by them. She was reg-ularly the target of ritual insult or stories of derision by the girls at lunch or in the midst of games. While jumping rope by herself several feet from the group, she was targeted as the cause of players' missing a turn. When she was briefly permitted to turn the rope, she was told to quit because of her poor turning style. For several days she decided that jumping with the boys was a preferable alternative and also more fun, joining their group. Thus, although some features of the girls' group showed less hierarchical social organization than the boys', girls' practices of exclusion toward out-group members were more pronounced and provided a way of defining the boundaries of their play group.

DIRECTIVES AND PARTICIPATION IN A
GIRL-CONTROLLED MIXED-SEX GAME

At the end of April 1997, the fourth-grade boys in this study had lit-tle experience with jump rope and generally participated as onlookers to the girls' game, commenting on their activity. In the first series of exam-ples, I examine five girls from April 28th, Emi, Lonnie, Janis, Sarah, and Kesha (a group that includes two Japanese Americans, two Whites, and one African American) jump while three boys (one African American and two Whites), Kevin, Stephen, and Ron, are standing on the periphery watch-ing the game. When observing the girls, one of the onlookers states that it had been 3 years since he had jumped rope. Another complimented the girls on the extraordinary skill required for the intricate moves of the girls occurring during the Texaco Mexico rhyme. After Kesha executed acro-batic movements in space, Kevin, who was exceptional in the boys' group for his jump rope skills, stated, "I Kesha, I cannot do that." At the same time that boys provided positive assessments of the girls' jump roping, they distanced themselves from the activity. In initial sessions watching the girls, the boys ridiculed the chantlike quality of the rhymes using exag-gerated sing-song intonation and mimicked the dancelike movements of the jumpers preparing to jump into a turning rope with exaggerated up-and-down head and arm movements. This activity, however, was ignored by the girls and treated as of no concern to them.

At Hanley School in spring of 1997 boys controlled who played on a team in the midst of games such as softball or soccer. Boys frequently made themselves the captains of the teams. When they picked players, girls were usually the last to be selected, and usually only a small number of girls, generally those who were friends with the captains, were selected to play.

Asymmetry in Directive Use

Jump rope provides a quite different story because the girls were the ones with the expertise in this activity. In orchestrating participation in jump rope during the April session, the girls used directives and responded to boys' requests to play in ways that demonstrated their control of the activity. Repetitively, the girls told the boys what the ground rules were when asked if they could play. Originally, Kevin, among the best jumpers of the boys, was scheduled to be the fourth jumper in the game. However, when he stated that he did not want to have to jump into the rope while it is turning and that he did not want to have to execute the complicated movements involved in Texaco Mexico (turning around, touching the ground, doing kicks and splits, and slapping the palm of a turner while "paying taxes"), three of the girls in the four-person girls' group told him that he could not play unless he did so.

Example 2[9] 4/28/97 11:48:08

```
 1  Kevin:      You're jumping in.
 2  Stephen:    No I ain't jumpin in.
 3  Janis:      You guys will have to jump with it.
 4  Emi:        You guys will have to jump in.
 5  Lonnie:     Yeah.
 6  Lonnie:     And Now! Now! ((preparing for Sarah
                to jump in))
 7  Kevin:     ⌈I don't wanna do that- Mexico Texaco.
 8  Lonnie/Em: ⌊Now! Now! Now! Now!
 9  Janis:      You have to.
10  Lonnie/Em:  Texaco ⌈Mexico
11  Kevin:             ⌊No I don't.
12  Janis:      Yes you do.
13  Lonnie/Em:  Where far away where they do some
                ((singing chant))
```

In response to Kevin's proposals (line 2) that he not have to jump into the rope while it is turning—or jump to a difficult rhyme—the girls counter that the move is obligatory with "You have to" (lines 3, 4, 5, 9) and a retort to Kevin's objection (line 12), "Yes you do." The girls state in no uncertain terms that particular moves have to be made by the boys if they are to play with the girls.

In example 3, Stephen displays his subordinate position vis-à-vis the girls by making a bid to enter the game through a mitigated request—"Can I try it?" (line 4):

Example 3 4/28/97 11:49:11

1	Stephen:	*((makes a nonverbal bid to join the group))*
2	Janis:	Stephen we're having a contest.
3		⌈ We're having a contest.
4	Stephen:	⌊ Can I try it?
5	Janis:	Well not <u>rea</u>lly because
6	Lonnie:	Because there's three against- one.

Inquiries by boys to the girls about joining the game are responded to with refusals. In example 3, opposition first occurs in response to a nonvocal bid with the account from Janis: "Stephen we're having a contest." Next in response to "Can I try it?" Janis states in line 5, "Well not <u>rea</u>lly"; her utterance is completed by an account from Lonnie: "Because there's three against- one" (line 6).

In example 4 (the continuation of example 3), two boys, Kevin and Stephen, make a second bid to enter the game through a request again phrased in a mitigated form: "Can you guys just- turn the rope?" Although initially Janis (line 2) grants permission, she quickly retracts it when one of her teammates argues that game should be exclusively for the girls: "No:: us" (line 4).

Example 4 4/28/97 11:49:30

1	Kevin:	Can you guys just- turn the rope?
		eh heh-heh!
2	Janis:	Okay <u>fine</u>. You can <u>play</u>.
		You can play. You can
		⌈ <u>play</u>.
3	Stephen:	⌊ (Hey. Can I play if I?)
4	Emi:	No:: <u>us</u>. *((shaking head))*
5	Kevin:	I don't want to do that
		⌈ Mexico thing
6	Janis:	⌊ Oh <u>yeah</u>. =You're not part of our gang.
		So you can't.

In response to her teammate's objection, Janis revises her prior granting of permission to play with first a change of state token—"Oh yeah."—followed by an account that expands on Emi's turn (line 4) arguing for the exclusivity rather than inclusiveness of the game: "You're not part of our gang. So you can't" (line 6). The girls agree to prohibit boys from playing the game.

A form of asymmetry exists with respect to the obligatory nature of rules. In example 5, 2½ min after Janis insisted that the boys had to jump into the moving rope to execute the acrobatic moves of Texaco Mexico (example 2), she herself encounters difficulty in executing the move. While the boys are watching the girls jump, Janis argues that she herself is not bound by the rule and can jump to whatever rhyme she wants to. In example 5, when she misses after one jump to Texaco Mexico, she states, "I don't want Texaco Mexico." Although at first a turner argues that Janis's turn is over ("Okay, Emi's turn," line 4), Janis rejects the statement that it is someone else's turn and stands on the rope so that it cannot be moved (line 5). Another player then proposes an easier rhyme that does not entail turning around or performing acrobatic moves while the rope is in motion: "Ice Cream Soda then" (line 6). When Emi next proposes that it is Kevin's turn (line 7), Janis holds out for getting another turn; she provides a dramatically executed counter with her polarity marker "No" and repeats Sarah's proposed replacement rhyme "Ice Cream Soda" in a pleading gesture with her hands extended.

Example 5 4/28/97 11:50:48

		((*Janis misses her jump as she begins to jump into the rope during Texaco Mexico*))
1	Turners:	Texaco Mexico
2	Janis:	Yeuw! ((*Janis misses—unsuccessfully jumping after her first jump*))
3		I don't want Texaco Mexico.
4	Lonnie:	Okay. Emi's turn. Emi's turn. ((*looking toward Emi*))
5	Janis:	No. I don't want Texaco Mexico. ((*stands on the rope so that they cannot start turning for a new person*))
6	Sarah:	Ice cream soda then.

7	Lonnie:	It's Kevin's turn. Kevin's turn.
8	Janis:	No. Ice Cream Soda *((does a pleading gesture with hands extended intensifying her action))*
9		Ice Cream <u>So</u>da guys.
10		Not loud cuz-
11		*((Girls turn for Janis as she jumps))*

An asymmetrical situation of power develops; the rules invoked by girls for boys as mandatory are ignored by the very girls who articulate their obligatory nature.

The girls display their control of the game not only by rejecting the boys' bids to play with them; in addition, the girls make decisions about an activity the following day, a volleyball game, which would involve the participation of the boys, without even consulting them. With an inclusive "Let's," Emi addresses the girls: "Hey you guys. Let's still have a contest with them."

Example 6 4/28/97 11:49:49

1	Emi:	Hey you guys. Let's still have a contest with them. *((looking at her teammates))*
2	Kevin:	(I would never ever let you call me)
3	Alan:	( )
4	Emi:	We're having a contest with you tomorrow for volleyball.
5		Okay. Bye. *((waves them away))*
6	Janis:	Bye. We don't want you any more.
7	Sarah:	How many turns do we get. *((boys move away))*

In example 6, line 4, without any input whatsoever from the boys, Emi informs them that the girls and boys are having a volleyball contest together the next day. Following the giving of this directive, the girls tell the boys to leave, through initiating the ritual closing moves of an encounter in line 5; they wave while stating, "Okay. Bye." One of the girls provides an explicit account for why the boys should leave: "We don't want you any more" (line 6). This account depicts the girls' desires rather than the requirements of the current activity[10] and thus constitutes among the most aggravated ways of formulating a directive (Ervin-Tripp, 1982).

The account that Janis provides argues quite forcefully that on this occasion girls control who can play. When the boys return 15 sec later, now agreeing to the girls' conditions for being a part of the activity—stating that they will execute the difficult moves of Texaco Mexico—Janis once more rejects their bid to join the game.

Example 7 4/28/97 10:50:16

> *((Boys return arguing that they want to play))*
>
> Alan: Alright. We (will) have to do that Texaco
>   Mexico. eh heh heh
> Janis: Well we don't <u>want</u> you to.
> Emi: Go::. Go:::.
> *((The girls continue to jump,*
> *ignoring the boys.))*

Through their actions, the girls define when they will play with the boys and patrol the borders and boundaries of their play space (Thorne, 1993).

Controlling a Peripheral Girl's Entry Into the Game

Continuously, girls respond with denials to the boys' requests to play. Bids to join the game are made not only by boys, but also by girls who are peripheral to the play group. In example 8, girls also reject a bid to join the activity made by Kristell, an African American girl who sometimes has lunch with Janis's group but does not regularly play with them. The bid to join is made by asking about who is the last person in line to jump.

Example 8 4/28/97 7 11:53:20

1 Kristell: Who's- last.
2 Emi: Uh- one of them is last *((does a large hand wave in direction of boys on the sidelines))*
3 Emi: Nobody's- Nobody's last.
4 Emi: ⌈Nobody's last.
5 Janis: ⌊Nobody's last.
6 Kristell: *((body deflates))*
7 (Boy):   (Kevin Go.)
8 Janis: This is kind of like a <u>con</u>test.
9 Kristell: Oh. Okay. *((looks away))*

Here Kristell's inquiry "Who's- last" is interpreted as a bid to play with the girls; asking about the appropriate turn order is only relevant for those who might be participating in the game. The girls forestall Kristell's positioning herself in the lineup by responding that there is no "last" position. Although the girls do not state overtly that Kristell cannot play, they effectively imply it through their "Nobody's last" response (lines 3–5). Because the person who is last is not known, it is impossible to find a place for Kristell in the game. By way of a second account, the girls state that they are having a contest (effectively one that excludes her). The account the girls give to Kristell is more indirect than the explanations given the boys (she is not told they do not want her); nevertheless, it functions in a similar way to exclude her and is treated as a rejection by Kristell, as evidenced by the deflation of her body (line 6) following the girls' refusal to let her play and by her walking away from the game 2 min later.

Shifting Participation Framework While Maintaining Control

For 6 min the game is played exclusively by girls. Then, in the midst of the girls' jump rope session, the participation structure suddenly shifts from one excluding the boys to one that includes them. In the midst of a dispute between the turners and Lonnie (the jumper) about the direction the rope is to be turned (toward or away from the jumper), Sarah (a turner) suddenly drops the rope to the ground and begins wiggling it (line 9). The dispute stops. Subsequently, through the use of requests and inclusive directives using the modal "can" and the inclusive "Let's," the girls decide to play a game called "snake." In this game, children must jump across the rope as it is wiggling close to the ground. The participation framework suddenly shifts from one in which girls alone were participants to one that is open for anyone to play:

Example 9 4/28/97 11:56:40

((*The girls have been turning the rope*
toward the jumper making it difficult
for Lonnie to jump in.))

1 Lonnie: Other way Sarah!
2 Janis: You guys.
3 Lonnie: Emi, I don't do that to you.

4	Sarah:	Emi- Lonnie. That's what you did to me
5		⌈ And I didn't like it either.
6	Emi:	⌊ I know.
7	Lonnie:	I know but then, ((sigh))
8		I never did it on Emi's turn.
9	Sarah:	((Sarah begins to wiggle the rope on the ground. and then Emi sits down and joins her in wiggling the rope))
10	Sarah:	La de dah de
11	Emi:	Now. Can we do snake?
12	Sarah:	Yeah.
13	Lonnie:	But this does not count as one of my turns.
14		Anyone could do this.
15		((Boys go across wiggling rope))
16	Sarah:	Let's play a game of snake.
17		No wait! Till we play a game of snake!
18	Emi:	A game of snake. Anyone could play.

The new activity initiated by Sarah with her wiggling movement of the rope on the ground (line 9) and Emi's subsequent request (line 11) "Can we do snake?" is ratified by others, through Lonnie's "Anyone could do this" (line 14) and Sarah's "Let's play a game of snake" (line 16). The course of the game now shifts, and the participation framework becomes more open, allowing the boys to play. Directives using modals and "Let's" are used at major junctures in an activity to suggest new alignments of participants and seek ratification from others. They propose rather than order.

Girls make the decisions about the activity. In example 10, a continuation of example 9, Emi suggests what a new course of action could consist of through her request "Can we try like limbo or something" (line 7). Girls specify which side of the rope girls and boys should be on as they divide up into teams (lines 1, 2, 6) and tell the boys to hold the ends of the rope:

Example 10 4/28/97 11:57:17

1	Sarah:	KAY! GIRLS ON THIS SIDE,
2	Lonnie:	Girls on this side,
3	Janis:	Here. Get it!
		((referring to the end of the rope))
4	Kevin:	What the heck is it.

5	Janis:	ONE BOY! HERE! Hold the end.
		Hold it! *((throwing rope to Kevin and pointing))*
6	Lonnie:	BOYS ON <u>THAT</u> SIDE!
		Get on the other <u>side</u>.
7	Emi:	⌈ Can we try like limbo or something.
8	Sarah:	⌊ *((kicks Andrew, then pushes him))*
9	Lonnie:	Okay! (Can we get)
10	Janis:	Only- no only- the girls!
11	Lonnie:	<u>Lim</u>bo!
12	Lonnie:	⌈ We're playing <u>Lim</u>bo!
13	Andrew:	⌊ *((begins to do wiggling of rope*
		as grabs it))
14	Janis:	Oh LIMB⌈O::!.
15	Kevin:	⌊ Limbo!
16	Andrew:	De op! de wat! de wat! *((sings and does*
		dance turning around, changing framework))
17	Lonnie:	We're playing Limbo!
18	Emi:	Lonnie get out!
19	Lonnie:	Okay! You saw- Tie! Limbo!
20	Emi:	I'm not holding the other end.
21		I kept on holding it.
22	Lonnie/Ja:	KEVIN. HOLD IT!
23		*((several people talk simultaneously))*
24	Emi:	It has to be one girl one boy hold
25		the ends of this. Each for a snake.

In organizing the activity, the girls make use of the most aggravated form of directives, bald imperatives: "Here! Get it!" "One boy- here. Hold this!" (lines 3, 5); "KEVIN. HOLD IT!" (line 22); "It has to be one girl one boy hold the ends of this" (line 24). For the most part, girls agree with each others' directives, affirming a particular version of the game. Differences of opinion regarding what the next stage of the game should consist of are short-lived. Sarah, Lonnie, and Emi affirm that the game of snake is open to anyone who wants to play, and Janis's (line 10) proposal is not upheld. When Lonnie subsequently invokes an alternative game, Limbo (lines 11 and 12), and boys begin to dance and sing "Deop de wat!" this suggestion is, by way of contrast, immediately taken up by Janis (line 14).

With the switch to Limbo, boys become participants rather than mere onlookers. Despite the boys' change in participation status, nevertheless, it is the girls who shape the event through their directives. Although girls exclude, counter, and command boys, boys ratify the girls' position of authority by posing requests to them. Moreover, when the girls are displeased with the way a move is being executed, they push boys who are turners, swing the beaded ends of the rope like a lasso in their direction, or chase them; boys, however, do not initiate similar physical moves toward girls. The girls' superior position with respect to knowing the game entitles them to dictate how it will be played.

DIRECTIVE USE IN A MIXED-GROUP CONTEST

During the weeks following the initial session the boys had with the girls, the boys practiced during recess and eventually became quite skilled in jump rope, with the exception of jumping to the rhyme Texaco Mexico, a rhyme that involves fancy footwork with the rope. At lunch, the girls talked excitedly about the fact that the boys also were interested in playing rope and made guesses about which boy would be first to run for the rope after lunch. For the most part, the boys pursued their own game apart from the girls. However, Angela, a girl who was treated as an outcast by both girls and boys, would on occasion join the boys; on such occasions, the girls said Angela was "flirting."

Boys' Decision Making

On May 29, 1 month after the initial session of boys attempting to join the girls' group in jump rope, as seven boys and seven girls are jumping in separate groups but near each other, the idea for a tournament arises. Angela approaches the boys' group and says, "We'll racing against you two." She is quickly ratified by one of the boys, Malcolm, a boy whom with Ron is the most experienced jumper; Malcolm subsequently provides his definition of the shape of the tournament—one in which only two of the boys (the best jumpers) rather than the entire group of seven will be competing.

Example 11 5/29/97 11:50:51

Angela: Okay, We'll racing against you two.
Malcolm: Okay. Me and Ron versus two- (.) girls.
           Two girls versus two of the boys.

Although in the April 28 encounter between girls and boys, girls made most of the decisions and boys made requests to the girls, on this occasion the boys have considerably more say in what takes place. The two best jumpers, Malcolm and Ron, initiate many of the decision-making moves. They assert their position of authority through issuing directives (examples 12, 13) and metastatements about the event (example 13).

Example 12 5/29/97 12:00

               ((After the girls have practiced several
               minutes the following occurs))
Malcolm: All the girls go bye bye.
Girls: *((Girls start to move to another area))*
Malcolm: Okay. Now the boys get to practice.
Ron: This is our home field.

Example 13 5/29/97 12:01:24

Malcolm: The contest is going nowhere fast.
            Start the event.

Both girls and boys ratify Malcolm and Ron's position of authority by posing questions to them.

Example 14 5/29/97 11:57:56

Kesha: Malcolm are we gonna use one rope?
Malcolm: *((nods))*
Kesha: We're using one rope.

Example 15 5/29/97 12:02:59

Michael: Ron. I'm the manager and the- and the-
           the judge. Okay?
Lyle: Screw you. Go away *((play-kicks Michael))*

Although Malcolm and Ron make the more important decisions of the game, two boys, Lyle and Jack, boys with considerably less skill in jumping rope who frequently end up turning the rope, play the role of gatekeepers regarding the group boundaries. They tell those who are not ratified participants to leave or where to locate themselves in space. In addition they define their addressees as "problems."

Example 16 5/29/97 11:58:24

Lyle: IF YOU'RE NOT IN THE TOURNAMENT
        GO OVER THERE SOMEWHERE!

Example 17 5/29/97 11:58:35

Jack: If you are not
Lyle: IF YOU'RE NOT IN THE COMPETITION
        GO OVER THERE!

Example 18 5/29/97 12:00:10

Jack: Come on! You and Karl are the
            biggest problem.
            Too many people around here.
Malcolm: Jack. Leave him alone.
            What's he doing wrong.

Example 19 5/29/97 12:02:00

Jack: Karl, Stephen, Tom.
        Is it such a hard decision.
        Stay behind the tree.
        Now you can watch.
        But stay behind the way of the tree.

Example 20 5/29/97 12:03:37

Jack: Tom. Where you are right now is perfect.
        Okay?
Tom: Jack. Does it really matter where I am?

Example 21 5/29/97 12:03:15

Jack: You guys wanna jump rope.
        There's too many people in this rope.
Tom: Jack. If there's too many people
        why don't you leave

Negotiation While Specifying Group Boundaries

Malcolm and Ron initially specify that the game will be played with four girls and four boys: "Okay we need a cot- the four goils." Six girls (Emi, Lonnie, Kesha, Janis, Sarah, and Lisa) then all state that they want to be the four girls in a highly competitive exchange. The intensity with which the girls raise their hands pleading to be among the contestants is mimicked by Malcolm (line 12) next. Because only a limited number of girls are going to play, extensive bidding for the positions among the girls ensues, and one player, Janis (the girl who had been the person responsible 1 month earlier for the boys' initial dismissal from the game) leaves in tears after she is asked by her girlfriends if she thinks she could actually beat the boys.

Example 22 5/29/97 11:55:13

1	Malcolm:	Okay we need a cot- the four goils.
2	Ron:	We need the four girls.
3	Kesha:	Me, Emi,
4	Emi:	Okay. I'm one of the four girls.
5	Malcolm:	It's an authentic way.
6	Emi:	I'M ONE OF THE
		⌈ FOUR GIRLS.
7	Lisa:	⌊ Lonnie
8	Lonnie:	I'm
		⌈ one.
9	Lisa:	⌊ I'm one.
10	Kesha:	I'm one of the four girls.
11	Janis:	⌈ I'm one.
12	Malcolm:	⌊ I'm one of em.
		((raising hands and mimicking gestures))
13	Emi:	Then get i(hh)n. ((looking at Lisa))
14	Janis:	⌈ I'm one of-
15	Lisa:	⌊ You said four.
16	Emi:	I know. I told-
17		I'm one of the four girls
		⌈ who's gonna come in.
18	Lisa:	⌊ Oh.
19		Oh. I am too!

20	Janis:	⌈ I want to. *((hands up))*
21	Lonnie:	⌊ I am. *((hands up))*
22	Kesha:	Janis. Do you think you could beat one of the boys?
23	Janis:	*((goes away crying))*

Although the boys ask the girls to specify who is on their team, no reciprocal action is initiated by the girls to the boys. However, both boys and girls join in ridiculing the outcast girl, Angela. In example 23, when Ron asks which girls are on the team, Lisa specifies that Angela is not (line 3). When Ron then tells the girls to eliminate Angela (line 4), Lisa tells her directly that she is not playing on the team: "Angela go out. You're not in this" (line 5). This leads to an extensive dispute between Angela and Lisa in which argumentative moves are prefaced with polarity markers (lines 6, 7, 9), among the most aggravated types of dispute turn initiators, and Lisa issues threats to Angela, which are answered by "so what" responses. The boys further insult Angela by stating that she should "work on her jumping" (line 22), although she is one of the best jumpers among them.

Example 23 5/29/97 11:56:36

1	Ron:	Who's on the team. You, you, you, *((pointing to Kesha, Lisa, Lonnie))*
2	Kesha:	Emi and Lonnie.
3	Lisa:	She's NOT. *((referring to Angela))*
4	Ron:	I know. So get her out of here.
5	Lisa:	Angela go out. You're not in this.
6	Angela:	Yes I am.
7	Lisa:	No you're not.
8	Angela:	If you guys can be in it then I can.
9	Lisa:	No you're not.
10	Angela:	Well I'm not leaving the rope.
11	Malcolm:	Look. There's a jump rope right there!
12	Lisa:	We'll go tell on you then.
13	Angela:	Tell!
14	Lisa:	There's five people allowed in the rope.
15		and we're five people.
16	Angela:	Tell. I don't really care. Tell.

17 Malcolm: Karl. He's not complaining about anything.
18   Tom you're the only stubborn one.
19 Lisa: Reggie-
20 Lisa: Well Reggie- ((calling a playground aide))
21 Ron: Next time you'll be in the competition.
22   Work on your jumping.
23 Angela: I <u>know</u> how to jump.
24 Malcolm: Look. It's wasting all our time.

In contrast to Janis, who leaves crying when she is told she cannot be
on the team, Angela holds her own, coming back with counters to each
imperative and exclusionary statement made by Lisa. Further imperatives
are delivered to her 1 min later by boys as well as girls (lines 1, 4, 5),
although this time she stands silently ignoring them.

Example 24 5/29/97 11:57:26

                   ((throughout the following Angela stands
                   motionless))
1   Lisa: Move Angela.
2   Lyle: Are you in the competition Angela?
3   Lisa: No. She's not.
4   Lyle: Then MOVE! It's a competition.
5   Go get another rope to jump.
6   Malcolm: Look. There's one
                  ⌈right there!
7   Lisa: ⌊REGGIE! I'm gonna go tell on her.
8   Boy: Kesha!

In numerous ways they degrade her. Later, when she does get a
chance to jump, they tell her to get to the end of the line.

Example 25 5/29/97 12:06:09

Angela: I'll jump with Raymond.
Ron: NO!
Lonnie: NO! You gotta go to the back of the line.
          Angela.
Angela: Well don't yell at me okay?

Girls' Decision Making

While the boys make many of the decisions, power is not completely in the hands of the boys. The girls decide two critical features of the game: (a) how girls will compete with boys and (b) what rhyme will be used. At the onset, multiple people are jumping simultaneously. Malcolm argues that teams of two boys and two girls should compete in the rope simultaneously (line 3).

Example 26 5/29/97 11:59:20

```
                ((Multiple players are jumping at once and
                having a problem jumping more than one time.))
 1  Malcolm:    Then there're too many people.
 2              It should be two-
 3              It should be like two of the boys vers
                two of the girls.
 4  Emi:        Hey Kesha do you wanna be- in one- one-
 5              um of the events?
 6  Malcolm:    Me and Ron together.
 7  Emi:        The other side.
 8  Emi:        No.
              ⌈ Okay.= We're four girls. Whoever has
 9  ( )       ⌊ I wanted(        )
10              We're four girls.
              ⌈ Whoever's last-
11  Kesha:    ⌊ Because he just told me to get in
12              and I didn't know we were
              ⌈ jumpin yet.
13  Emi:      ⌊ GET OUT!
14  Emi:        OKAY. LIS:::TE:::N!
15  Jack:       Bye, bye bye. ((pushing Karl))
16  Emi:        We're (.) four (.) gi(hh)rls.
17  Sarah:    ⌈ The other four girls ((dancing, chanting))
18           ⌊ Whoever
19  Emi:        WHOEVER (.) GOES (.) LAST (.)
20              VERSUS whoever's
21              best on your team::.
```

22 Ron: We have.
23 Kesha: It should be one at a time.
24 Malcolm: It should be two-
               it could be one boy, one girl.

Malcolm's proposal that two boys should compete against two girls is countered by Emi (line 14), who yells loudly over the others' talk her vision of the contest as one between teams of one boy and one girl rather than two against two, as Malcolm had suggested. After Kesha ratifies this proposal ("It should be one at a time," line 23), Malcolm (line 24) revises his original designation of two against two (line 3) to "one boy, one girl." The intonation that Emi uses in lines 16 and 19, with micropauses after each word, adds to the directness of her statement.

As four girls are jumping simultaneously during a practice session before the official tournament, the boys start turning the rope fast, as if the event were speed jumping. Kesha yells at the boys for going too fast and tells them the rhyme that will be used. This is important, in that the Texaco Mexico rhyme the girls select is one they are expert in.

Example 27 5/29/97 12:00:37

   ((Boys turn rope rapidly))
Kesha: GO SLOWLY.
         WE'RE DOING TEXACO MEXICO.
         DON'T GO SO FAST!

During the first real event in the contest, Malcolm asks the girls to confirm his idea that the event is speed jumping. However, Emi (lines 3, 6) and Kesha (line 5) counter his proposal that the event is speed jumping by saying that the event is Texaco Mexico.

Example 28 5/29/97 12:04:21

1 Raymond: Malcolm. Go in with Emi.
2 Malcolm: What's this one. It's speed jumping?
3 Emi: ⌈NO:::,
4 Lisa: ⌊What is ⌈this.
5 Kesha: ⌊It's Texaco Mexico.
6 Emi: No who could- who could get-
              Texaco Mexico the longer.

Thus, although boys organize the game through imperatives throughout the jump rope session, girls define who will jump against whom and what form of jumping will take place. They win against every contest between a girl and boy when Texaco Mexico is the rhyme being jumped to and celebrate their victories with hand slaps, victory signs, and loud scorekeeping. After several rounds of jumping to the rhyme Texaco Mexico, the game becomes more chaotic as the contest shifts to speed jumping, with several people in the rope simultaneously (the boys' favorite event) and new girls who are not expert jumpers joining the contest. Eventually, the boys gain ground and win by 2 points.

CONCLUSIONS

The SWH proposes that because boys and girls grow up in different subcultures, they learn to "do different things with words in a conversation" (Maltz & Borker, 1982, p. 200) as a result of "the very different social contexts" in which they interact in segregated sex–gender arrangements. Alternative styles of communication are related to subcultural differences based on gender and can lead to miscommunication.

In the analysis presented here, boys and girls participating in a similar activity, organizing participation in a game, have no difficulty understanding the moves of one another. Both boys and girls make use of similar types of speech acts. The middle-class 10-year-old girls in this study demonstrated their ability to use bald imperatives—acts that are similar for organizing game activity across sex–gender groups—and speech forms I earlier (Goodwin, 1980) analyzed as characteristic of a masculine organizational style. What differentiates this study from my earlier work (which Maltz & Borker drew on) is that the context (Sheldon, 1996) is not the organization of task activity in a neighborhood play group, but rather the coordination of activity in a game on the playground. The organization of girls' task activity such as making rings from glass bottles, contained little role specialization, and tasks could be completed individually. In games such as jump rope, by way of contrast, there was more role differentiation and a premium on limiting size of the group; the more limited the number of participants, the more frequently one gets to jump.

The way in which jump rope is played demonstrates that the relative skill level of participants is important in determining who has the power to define the rules of the game. In the April 28 play session, boys initially displayed their subordinate status vis-à-vis the girls by making requests to join the activity. Refusing their requests, girls, by way of contrast, issued imperatives and directed counter moves to the boys. The girls told them they could not play, using accounts such as "We don't want you any more." When the girls shifted the game to "snake" and Limbo and included the boys in their play, they still maintained control of the play activity, defining who had to hold the ends of the rope and where teams of boys and girls would stand.

In the mixed group situation 1 month later, after they had gained skill in the game, boys had considerably more voice in the organization of the activity. Two boys who were expert in jumping emerged as leaders and were ratified as having control over many features of the activity—organizing practice before the event, determining the timing of the event, deciding how many ropes were to be used, and selecting players. Other less skilled (yet ingroup) players assumed the role of gatekeeper—telling boys who were unratified participants with bald imperatives where to go and what to do. The decisions the girls made—determining how many players from different teams would jump simultaneously and what type of jumping would be used in the contest—were important (in that they favored the girls' jumping style) but more limited.

In both the jump rope sessions examined here excluding outgroup members, an activity commonly associated with female social organization (Douvan & Adelson, 1966; Eder & Hallinan, 1978; Feshbach & Sones, 1971), constitutes a feature of the interaction. In the initial phase of the April jump rope session, girls refused permission to boys and a girl who was not a member of their clique. The account they provided to the girl—that they were in the midst of a contest—was less direct than the account they gave the boys: "We don't want you any more." In the May jump rope contest, boys created a clear separation between participants and onlookers through utterances (primarily directed at boys) such as "IF YOU'RE NOT IN THE TOURNAMENT GO OVER THERE SOME-WHERE!" Although both boys and girls used aggravated, face-threatening directives to an outcast girl, they did not direct such actions to boys.

In other work (Goodwin 1990, 1997), I argued for the relevance of studying speech activities longitudinally. Ethnographically based studies that provide a form of time depth permit us to examine how the social orchestration of an activity can change over time. With practice, boys became more skilled and were no longer in a position of subordination with respect to girls. Boys began to use the aggravated directive style of girls when they become more proficient in the game. Both girls and boys can make use of a variety of directive forms; the use of imperative forms and aggravated counter moves is related to acquired skill. Rather than being sex linked, features of language use may be closely related to one's achieved position in a specific context, a finding resonate with that made by O'Barr and Atkins (1980) in their analysis of language in an American trial courtroom.

With the development of more playground activities in which girls' games—for example, the highly competitive game of double dutch, which is featured in international athletic competitions—rather than boys' games are promoted, I hope increased opportunities for girls to interact in competitive ways that permit them to develop their abilities as powerful actors in cross-sex interaction will come.

NOTES

1   Harding's (1975) study of gender relations among rural Spanish villagers found that although men worked in agricultural tasks and public arenas, engaging in economic negotiations and political argument, women were concerned with more private realms that involved gossip within networks of friends and relatives.

2   In making this claim, Maltz and Borker (1982) cited work by Brooks-Gunn and Matthews (1979), who argued that "a major feature of most middle-childhood peer groups is homogeneity in gender composition" (p. 203).

3   DeHart (1996) reviewed research on gender-specific linguistic interaction patterns in preschoolers' peer groups; she argued that by age 5 "girls' discourse has consistently been characterized as collaborative and mitigated, whereas boys' peer discourse has been characterized as controlling and unmitigated" (p. 81).

According to Miller, Danaher, and Forbes (1986), who investigated conflicts among racially and socioeconomically mixed 5- to 7-year-old children, boys are more forceful in pursuing their own agendas than girls; girls were more concerned with maintaining group harmony and made use of strategies that mitigated rather than provoked conflict. Leaper (1991), looking at middle- to upper middle-class children ages 4 to 9 found that girls used more speech acts that demonstrate "mutual coordination, responsivity and elaboration" (p. 800) compared to boys, whose speech acts were frequently insults, orders, and refutations. Examining the pretend play of 4-year-olds with siblings, DeHart (1996) found that "children's use of mitigated and unmitigated forms with siblings is not the same as that reported for peers" (p. 92). See also Sheldon (1996, p. 58) for further citations of work on gender and conflict.

4 Before beginning my study, I explained to both parents (through a letter and during a parent–teacher meeting) and children (whom I told in person) in the school my interest in activities children organized among themselves apart from adults; on each occasion of videotaping at play during recess and at lunch, I asked the children's permission to film them. In that it is not uncommon for researchers to be videotaping the children in other contexts, the children were quite accustomed to the videocamera.

5 Similar to what Thorne (1993) described, the largest area of the playground, the playing fields, were occupied primarily by boys.

6 One of the coaches believed that the group of boys who played jump rope chose that activity so that they could interact with the girls.

7 During 1998 and 1999, the game was not taught in physical education and I seldom saw girls playing it.

8 The rhyme for Texaco Mexico is as follows:

Texaco Mexico went over the hill and far away
Where they do some kicks, kicks, kicks,
And they do some splits, splits splits,
And they turn around round round
And they touch the ground, ground,
And they pay their taxes, taxes, taxes,
And they get outa town, town, town.

9 Each example includes the date the interaction was recorded and the time.

10 Among the African American children I studied in Philadelphia (Goodwin, 1990), boys' directives rather than girls' frequently dealt with personal desires rather than requirements of the activity.

REFERENCES

Adler, P. A., Kless, S. J., & Adler, P. (1992). Socialization to gender roles: Popularity among elementary school boys and girls. *Sociology of Education, 65,* 169–187.

Bellinger, D. C., & Gleason, J. B. (1982). Sex differences in parental directives to young children. *Sex Roles, 8,* 1123–1139.

Borman, K. M. (1982). *Children's interpersonal relationships: Playground games and social cognitive skills, final report.* Washington, DC: National Institute of Education.

Borman, K. M., & Frankel, J. (1984). Gender inequities in childhood: Social life and adult work life. In K. M. Borman, D. Quarm, & S. Gideonse (Eds.), *Women in the workplace: Effects on families* (pp. 113–135). Norwood, NJ: Ablex.

Brooks-Gunn, J., & Matthews, W. S. (1979). *He and she: How children develop their sex-role identity.* Englewood Cliffs, NJ: Prentice Hall.

Brown, P., & Levinson, S. C. (1978). Universals of language usage: Politeness phenomena. In E. N. Goody (Ed.), *Questions and politeness: Strategies in social interaction* (pp. 56–311). Cambridge, England: Cambridge University Press.

DeHart, G. B. (1996). Gender and mitigation in 4-year-olds' pretend play talk with siblings. *Research on Language and Social Interaction, 29,* 81–96.

Douvan, E., & Adelson, J. (1966). *The adolescent experience.* New York: Wiley.

Eder, D., & Hallinan, M. T. (1978). Sex differences in children's friendships. *American Sociological Review, 43,* 237–250.

Eisenberg, A. R., & Garvey, C. (1981). Children's use of verbal strategies in resolving conflicts. *Discourse Processes, 4,* 149–170.

Ervin-Tripp, S. (1976). "Is Sybil there?": The structure of some American English directives. *Language in Society, 5,* 25–67.

Ervin-Tripp, S. (1982). Structures of control. In L. C. Wilkinson (Ed.), *Communicating in the classroom* (pp. 27–47). New York: Academic.

Farris, C. E. P. (2000). Cross-sex peer conflict and the discursive production of gender in a Chinese preschool in Taiwan. *Journal of Pragmatics, 32,* 539–568.

Feshbach, N., & Sones, G. (1971). Sex differences in adolescent reactions toward newcomers. *Developmental Psychology, 4,* 381–386.

Goodwin, M. H. (1980). Directive/response speech sequences in girls' and boys' task activities. In S. McConnell-Ginet, R. Borker, & N. Furman (Eds.), *Women and language in literature and society* (pp. 157–173). New York: Praeger.

Goodwin, M. H. (1990). *He-said-she-said: Talk as social organization among Black children.* Bloomington: Indiana University Press.

Goodwin, M. H. (1994). Ay chillona!: Stance-taking in girls' hop scotch. In M. Bucholtz, A. C. Liang, L. Sutton, & C. Hines (Eds.), *Cultural performance: Proceedings of the third Berkeley Women and Language Conference* (pp. 232–241). Berkeley, CA: Berkeley Women and Language Group.

Goodwin, M. H. (1997). Toward families of stories in context. *Journal of Narrative and Life History, 7,* 107–112.

Goodwin, M. H. (1998). Games of stance: Conflict and footing in hopscotch. In S. Hoyle & C. T. Adger (Eds.), *Kids' talk: Strategic language use in later childhood* (pp. 23–46). New York: Oxford University Press.

Gordon, D., & Ervin-Tripp, S. (1984). The structure of children's requests. In R. L. Schiefelbusch & J. Pickar (Eds.), *The acquisition of communicative competence* (pp. 298–321). Baltimore: University Park Press.

Harding, S. (1975). Women and words in a Spanish village. In R. Reiter (Ed.), *Towards an anthropology of women* (pp. 283–308). New York: Monthly Review Press.

Kyratzis, A., & Guo, J. (1996). "Separate worlds for girls and boys?" Views from U.S. and Chinese mixed-sex friendship groups. In D. Slobin, J. Gerhardt, A. Kyratzis, & J. Guo (Eds.), *Social interaction, social context, and language: Essays in honor of Susan Ervin-Tripp* (pp. 555–578). Mahwah, NJ: Lawrence Erlbaum Associates, Inc.

Labov, W., & Fanshel, D. (1977). *Therapeutic discourse: Psychotherapy as conversation.* New York: Academic.

Leaper, C. (1991). Influence and involvement in children's discourse: Age, gender and partner effects. *Child Development, 62,* 797–811.

Lever, J. (1976). Sex differences in the games children play. *Social Problems, 23,* 478–487.

Maccoby, E. E. (1990). Gender and relationships: A developmental account. *American Psychologist, 45,* 513–520.

Maltz, D. N., & Borker, R. A. (1982). A cultural approach to male–female miscommunication. In J. J. Gumperz (Ed.), *Communication, language and social identity* (pp. 196–216). Cambridge, England: Cambridge University Press.

Miller, P. M., Danaher, D. L., & Forbes, D. (1986). Sex-related strategies for coping with interpersonal conflict in children aged five and seven. *Developmental Psychology, 22,* 543–548.

O'Barr, W., & Atkins, S. (1980). "Women's language" or "powerless language"? In S. McConnell-Ginet, R. Borker, & N. Furman (Eds.), *Women and language in literature and society* (pp. 93–110). New York: Praeger.

Piaget, J. (1965). *The moral judgment of the child.* New York: Free Press. (Original work published 1932)

Sachs, J. (1987). Preschool boys' and girls' language use in pretend play. In S. Philips, S. Steele, & C. Tanz (Eds.), *Language, gender and sex in comparative perspective* (pp. 178–188). Cambridge, MA: Cambridge University Press.

Sheldon, A. (1992). Conflict talk: Sociolinguistic challenges to self-assertion and how young girls meet them. *Merrill-Palmer Quarterly, 38,* 95–117.

Sheldon, A. (1996). You can be the baby brother, but you aren't born yet: Preschool girls' negotiation for power and access in pretend play. *Research on Language and Social Interaction, 29,* 57–80.

Strayer, F. F., & Strayer, J. (1980). Preschool conflict and the assessment of social dominance. In D. R. Omark, F. F. Strayer, & D. G. Freedman (Eds.), *Dominance relations: An ethological view of human conflict and social interaction* (pp. 137–157). New York: Garland STPM.

Thorne, B. (1993). *Gender play.* New Brunswick, NJ: Rutgers University Press.

Wingard, L. (1998). *Directives in jump rope among boys.* Paper prepared for University of California at Los Angeles Applied Linguistics class, Discourse Analysis.

Research on Language and Social Interaction, 34(1), 107–130

Classroom "Families": Cooperating or Competing— Girls' and Boys' Interactional Styles in a Bilingual Classroom

Jenny Cook-Gumperz
Graduate School of Education
University of California

Margaret Szymanski
Xerox Palo Alto Research Center

This article examines how students use gendered discourse practices in small peer group settings to accomplish their school tasks. The analysis contributes to the separate worlds hypothesis by showing how Latino children interactionally orient to their peer group as a gendered context. For 1 academic year, observations were made in an elementary bilingual classroom. The target 3rd-grade teacher referred to her student groups as "families," a label that emerged as a legitimizing metaphor for the group's collective action. In cooperating and competing to accomplish their school tasks, the students strategically used Spanish and English. Further, the girls in the "family" adopted a brokering role to facilitate group cooperation much as they would in their actual families. For bilingual children, gender differences are played out within a cultural milieu created at the junctures of home and classroom and at the intersection of language and ethnic identity.

Although the separate worlds hypothesis (SWH) has been demonstrated in many different settings from children's interaction in peer groups to everyday exchanges between women and men, a key question

Correspondence concerning this article should be sent to Jenny Cook-Gumperz, Graduate School of Education, University of California, Santa Barbara, CA 93106. E-mail: cook-gumperz@education.ucsb.edu remains about how sharp the division is: To what extent does the hypothesis hold true across cultures and contexts? Gender is not an immutable given that has the same manifestations across different social groups and contexts; rather, it is an interactional accomplishment that develops from the specifics of everyday interactions. The questions that this article asks are what makes a significant difference? How do gender distinctions grow out of different context-specific discourse practices? To what extent do these discourse differences deepen into different ways of knowing that will in their turn influence many other activities?

There exists some form of family and kin grouping that collaborates and organizes gender roles in families in all societies. Children's gender experiences are defined and shaped in the context of these collectivities (Ortner, 1997). In other words, families provide essential contexts for developing the discourse of gendered behavior. Dunn and Plomin (1990) argued that families as the primary socializing site involve children in a relational dynamic from the moment of their births. Genetically similar individuals in a family grow into different human personalities. As each additional child is added to the family in a particular ordinal position, the relational dynamic is changed (Dunn & Plomin, 1990). By this logic, a firstborn boy encounters a different family context from that of a boy born into a family unit with an older sister; the same is true for girls who grow up in a family with brothers.

Although anthropologists have argued that firstborn children are unique, the significance of ordinal position is that it expands the matrix of possibilities for experiencing gender relations (Sulloway, 1996). What is more, we argue, the family composition makes available a different discursive space for each participant. More important, perhaps, childrens' experience of family provides at the very least a glimpse into others' gendered lives within the intimacy and emotional pressures that mark everyday family discourse (Cook-Gumperz, in press). Although each child encounters a slightly different gendered world, it is in the family that they also become aware of the possibility of opposition to the seeming determinacy of their own gender and ordinal position. Moreover, it seems likely that these early experiences may continue to shape actions in other worlds beyond the family.

Now consider the issue of how children participate in organized encounters in the world outside of the family. For most children, their first and most major socializing experience of a public world is entry into school where they meet unknown adults and other children, both peers as well as older and younger children (Cook-Gumperz, in press). In fact, the SWH begins with the school-age child. The overwhelmingly peer-centered relationships of school stand in strong contrast to the ordinality of the family that is both ordered by age and shaped by gendered complementarities. Research has shown that peer group experience outside of the family is considered to be the significant ground for children to explore their own understandings of gender (Lloyd & Duveen, 1992), because such social contexts provide more open possibilities than do the established relations of the family of origin. It is this latter position that provides the starting point for this study.

Research over the past decade or so shows that elementary schools provide group experiences that make for a gender awareness realized through conversational sparring, banter, and competition between the genders (Goodwin, 1990; Streeck, 1986; Thorne, 1993). Thorne (1993) found that in activities outside of the school on the playground, boys and girls establish boundaries between themselves that allow for limited cooperation yet foster competition at the borders. Within the classroom, competitive exchanges between boys and girls play out a politics of gender in the classroom that is characteristic of peer, school discourse (e.g., Kyratzis & Guo, 1996; Streeck, 1986). Streeck's (1986) study in an ethnically mixed classroom found that boys and girls formed gender-distinct and competing "teams" within single classroom workgroups. These competing teams were initiated by boys to exclude the girls' participation in work tasks. However, he also found that when the social context changed to a non-task-specific setting, the conversational exchanges became noncompetitive, and these same boys chatted freely with the girls. It would seem, therefore, that the importance of gender varies with context.

THE BILINGUAL CLASSROOM

Our Argument

This study takes place in a third-grade, predominantly bilingual, English–Spanish classroom in a central California school. In this bilingual classroom, a cooperative learning program is used to focus on literacy learning through reading and writing in English (Szymanski, 1996). During class, students are divided into what the teacher designates as "family" groups of four or five students working together at separate tables. The students in each group can organize their group's common tasks in any way that seems to promote collaboration between the participants, as they might in their own family life. Because no single speaker is given primary rights of speaking or is assigned a single organizer's role, each participant must compete for the floor, as children might in a family. The data for the study are taken from videotaped classroom sessions collected over the course of a school year by Szymanski, who in addition to observing, participated in some of the classroom tasks as a classroom aide. Because the data were collected over an entire school year, some of the same children appear in different work groupings.

Initially, we observed a greater amount of group collaboration on school tasks between girls and boys in the "family" designated groups than previous research had suggested might happen. Particularly, we noticed that girls played a larger organizational part and that when verbal sparring happened, it was most likely to occur between girls competing to control the group's activities. These initial findings present an opposite view to the more usual pattern of gender separation, or borderwork, that Thorne (1993) described: Boys and girls form separate groups that usually are distinguished by cooperative activities, provided they do not compete over boundary areas or activities. In a study of classroom talk, Swann (1988) showed that in situations such as these, of open conversation, boys are always the dominating force. Our observations are also at variance with the kind of gender competition between boys that has been documented extensively in classrooms and play yards (Goodwin, 2001; Thorne, 1993). We argue that designating the student group as a "family" and the frequent use of this term influences the organizational structure of the class. In addition, this metaphor provides access to a particular cultural agenda of gendered roles that differ from those more commonly associated with free classroom discourse. The teacher's labeling of each groups' collective action as "family activity" gives the students individually and collectively a legitimizing metaphor for claiming any of their actions as "working with their family." This warrant holds whether the action appears to be directly supportive of the group's tasks. Nonetheless, the underlying dynamic of the group discourse most often remains collaborative.

The term *family* as a label for a social grouping, we argue, provides a legitimizing metaphor for collaborative possibilities of a kind that have been shown to have significance in the life world of Latino children.

Ethnographic research indicates that Latino children experience a world outside of school that always involves both immediate and extended family relationships (Moll, Amanti, Neff, & Gonzales, 1992). Vasquez, Pease-Alvarez, and Shannon (1994), in a detailed ethnography of Mexican families in one neighborhood in a Northern California city, described children growing up in bilingual, family-oriented neighborhoods in which school-going children are placed in the role of translators and cultural brokers for both family and friends. By providing a guiding metaphor for framing specific classroom interaction such as "family," the classroom participation framework offers a potential script for the realization of gendered discourse that might differ from the more usual classroom borderwork patterns. Although girls and boys are likely to cooperate on tasks with the legitimating metaphor of family, girls are even more likely to play a main role in facilitating cooperation; that is, they act somewhat like organizing "elder sisters," making sure that all the other children participate in the activities. In contrasting the life of one fourth-grade girl, Leti, with the activities of her elder brother, Vasquez et al. (1994) commented as follows:

> She stayed closer to home and she was mostly involved with the activities of her large extended family who lived nearby such as weddings, birthdays, anniversaries, etc. . . . . Leti was being groomed to inherit the role of family translator from her older brother Adan, who no longer had the time or interest to continue translating for older Spanish-speaking family members. Consequently she came to accompany adults to doctors offices or places of employment. (p. 85)

In other words, it seems that although boys are often free to turn to outside activities, girls are expected to stay closely involved with family responsibilities on a day-to-day basis. The earlier comments provide an ethnographic glimpse of what it means for a school-age child who speaks English as a second language to become a cultural broker for her family.

The Vasquez et al. (1994) study illustrates a world in which children are involved with both Spanish and English, a world in which two languages remain a part of the student's family experience, their friendships, and their daily communicative practice in and outside of the home. English is the language of the outside world, and Spanish initially indexes the world of home and its values. As children become more active outside of the family, their communicative repertoire alters. The peer-group world of school-going children bridges the two domains. That is, both worlds are a relevant part of daily experience, and one or the other can be evoked strategically to accomplish particular communicative purposes. In this study, given the acceptance of "family" as a part of classroom organization, we hypothesize that Latina girls were likely to play a dominant organizational role in the dynamics of the group.

Although the teacher and the students share a bilingual repertoire, the classroom communicative context is English dominant. The students complete writing tasks in English, but as the examples later show, whereas the children read and formulate answers to questions in English, in their groups they are free to discuss and negotiate answers in either Spanish or English. As a part of the cooperative learning pedagogy, groups work together to explore mutually constructed answers, and in the process they build group-specific communicative practices (Szymanski, 1996).

In what follows, we present examples that show how the family metaphor makes available a particular communicative frame. We argue that this frame legitimizes a range of gendered performances in which "family members" not only help each other but also complain, argue, and compete for control of the floor to get tasks accomplished. The "family" framing for classroom communicative practice encourages students to adopt strategies of helping and collaborating that are directly counter to the gender-competitive stances more usual of middle childhood. In this way, we demonstrate some of the contextual limitations of the SWH.

The Communicative Context of the Classroom: Talk of "Family"

In the following set of examples, the naming of the group as a family by the teacher is picked up and used by students themselves. In this way, the teacher and students both invoke the term *family* as a named social category in establishing a classroom communicative context and as creating a warrant for any further conversational strategies. Although the students are aware that the "official" classroom language task requires them to talk and work in English, their varying use of Spanish and English takes on a variety of meanings such as signaling "we are doing our own business now" or distinguishing between formal classroom talk and private remarks.

In examples 1, 2, and 3, the teacher and teacher's aide invoke the notion of family to emphasize the need for group cooperation. The repeated use of expressions like "ask your family" serves as an indirect way of suggesting that the students need to collaborate in an environment in which all are free to give their opinions and help in completing the task at hand. In other words, naming the work group as a family is intended to reinforce the idea of shared group collaboration and provides a framework for classroom learning.

Example 1

1 T: get busy, your **family** needs you.

Example 2

1   ((to Loretta in answer to a request for help))
2 T: don't ask me. Ask your **family** if that looks
3   good to them.

Example 3
Background: Jorge (J) and Davina (D) are sitting on one side of the table, George (G) and Amelia (A) on the other. The teacher's aide (TA) responds to D's request for help

1 TA: well then pay attention to your (.) **family**,
2 G: eh- eh-
3 D: but lookit, they don't want to help (us-)

In examples 1, 2, and 3, the teacher and aide respond to off-task behavior and requests for help. Here, both adults draw a contrast between asking them for assistance and relying on "the family" group collaboration. Thus, for the teacher, the term *family* is synonymous with classroom cooperative group activities in the accomplishment of school tasks and is a primary source of help. However, for the students, the term *family* signals much more than the collaborative support intended by the teachers. Students also can express negative feelings or sibling rivalry through use of this term, as they do in example 4.

Example 4
Background: Davina (D) and Yolanda (Y) are sitting on one side of the table across from Sonia (S) and George (G). Y and G are writing answers to story questions as D looks around and sees S put her papers away as if she is finished with the task.

1 D: OU::, you havta **wait for your family**,
2   (0.4)
3 S: they STINK, **my family stinks**,
4 D: YOU: stink.
5   (0.2)
6 S: no. ((writes on her paper))

7   G: COO:L. ((laughs and erases))
8   D: let's get somebody SMART over here.

In example 4, Sonia answers Davina's request with the complaint "my family stinks." Her negative response sets off a verbal sparring sequence. The lone boy in the group, George, acts as a bystander and finds the argument amusing, much as a younger brother would. In example 4 as in example 5 next, the dynamics of gender shift according to the gender balance in the group. A lone boy is more likely to assume what we have called the younger brother role.

In example 5, the work group is engaged in the task of constructing written English comprehension questions to a story they have just read. As the students work, the teacher is overheard addressing the whole class on each individual group's progress, showing that she intends the term *family* to refer directly to any group that cooperates productively.

Example 5[1]
Background: George (G) and Daisy (D) are sitting across the table from Sonia (S) and Emman (E)

1   E: >yo voy a poner<
          I'm going to put
2   which school did Annie go,
3   S: what GRA:de (   )
4   G: oye, Sonia::
          listen
5   E: ⌈what grade ⌉
6   G: ⌊y luego qué⌋
          and then what
7   S: huh?
8   G: y luego qué de little.
          and then what for little.
9   T: ((to whole class)) **esta familia ya placti-**
                            this family already dis-
10   **está terminada con sus seis preguntas,**
          is finished with their six questions,
11   **tenemos tres terminados**
          we have three finished ((groups))
12   **dos trabajando junto**
          two working together

13   G: come O:n Sonia, little, ven
          come on
14   D: what grade annie qué
          what
15   S: ((looks at G's paper)) ya está
          that's it
16   G: así 'ra
          like this
17   E: which grade did Annie go
18   D: did the one
19   E: which school what- what school did Annie
20   go. what (1.0) what An- Annie (0.6)
21   how do Annie (.) {R>}cómo se sintió Annie
                          how did Annie feel
22   cuando ella estaba en la escuela {<R}
          when she was at school
23   (11.0) ((all continue writing in silence))

In example 5, the teacher employs Spanish to highlight her message about family collaboration by pointing to the groups that have finished as an example of functioning families. The teacher's use of Spanish implicitly reinforces the idea of family by linking it to the home context via language. Following the teacher's comments, the group continues working on their own to finish the questions. George tries to persuade Sonia to help him finish spelling the word "little," and her comment "that's it" on line 15 shows that she is an expert in the group. Emman repeats Daisy's question in line 17 and receives no response, so he reformulates the question in line 19. Still unanswered, he shifts into Spanish in line 21 with a different question, as if to strengthen his appeal for some response. It would appear that the students' idea of family collaboration in the classroom differs from that of the teacher, in that they see the family as a group of individuals who may or may not choose to collaborate. When the group collaborates, a girl is most likely to be the leader, giving the other group members assistance or refusing to do so.

Naming "Family" Activities: Helping

Within the classroom, members of family work groups are encouraged by the teacher to cooperate by helping each other, so that every participant gets the task finished. Thus, for teachers, the way that family collaboration is achieved is through "helping," which includes comments, quiet talk, and assistance by one student to another. From the teacher's point of view, helping activities should be demonstrably collaborative and focus on the group text-based tasks of reading and writing. However, when students take up this term, they use it to warrant any activity that involves one person taking a larger than usual interest in what another person is doing. Examples 6 and 7 show how for the students, labeling an event as "helping" serves as a ploy to legitimate any task-based activities, whether or not they encourage collaborative talk.

Example 6
Background: Joel is sitting at the next table, Davina sits beside Jorge, and George (G) and Amelia are sitting across from them.

1   G: ((to Joel)) estoy en la tres,
                 I'm on the third one,
2   I'm **helping** these guys,
3   >que no saben nada,<
         cuz they don't know anything
4   ((points to Davina and Jorge))

Example 7
Background: Sonia is standing beside the table where Jorge and Davina (D) are sitting across from George and Amelia when the teacher's aide (TA) sees her chatting with them.

1   TA: ((to Sonia)) I saw you (.) visiting,
2   D: no, she's our **helper**, she's our **helper**,
3   TA: **ask your family for help,**
4   D: but teacher, she's our **helper**,
5   TA: well, ⌈ **ask your family,**
6   D: ⌊ she comes around and **helps**,

In examples 6 and 7, the students use the term *helping* to refer to any peer group talk, even chatting, that occurs when a student visits another family. In example 7, the students make an ironic jest of the teacher's idea of the work group as a family, yet in so doing their communicative practice resembles the banter and jesting of family life. On the other hand, in example 7 when the teacher's aide sees Sonia, a member of another group, talking with Davina's group, she remarks in line 3 that they should rely on each other for help; thus, she agrees with the children's use of helping. The work group protests, suggesting that Sonia is there "to help them." In other words, they justify Sonia's presence by invoking the officially acceptable activity of helping. In both of these examples, the students use the teacher's label to justify their own activities. At the same time, their use of the term shows that they understand that "help" is meant to refer to collaboration in getting school tasks accomplished.

Students may also make a verbal game of the notion of helping and the idea of the group as a family, as in example 8. Here, Junior, a dominant English speaker, is Emman's partner. When Emman uses Spanish to ask Alicia for help and she responds in Spanish directing him to ask his partner Junior, not only do they exclude Junior from the conversation, but they make an ironic comment on the teacher's idea of collaboration in the group.

Example 8
George (G) and Alicia (A) sit across from Junior (J) and Emman (E)

```
1    E:    el número tres empieza
           number three starts
2    J:    you're supposed to- (      ) to do that
3    E:    ((to A)) pero dime::
                    but tell-me
4    A:    dile que te ayuda él, él es tu part[ner],
           tell him to help you, he's your partner
5    E:                                     [uh ] huh,
6          °Ms. Si:mon,°
7    A:    pues, yo no sé,
           well, I don't know,
8    J:    hello (.) HOW ((plays with microphone))
9    A:    look look ((refers to tape recorder at right))
10   G:    mira que pasa.
           look what's happening.
11   E:    cuál es la answe::r=
           what is
12   J:    =hello hello
13   A:    no te- no te voy a decir la answer,
           I'm not going to tell you the answer,
14   E:    somos una familia.
           we are a family.
```

15   A: y qué::?,
            so what::?,
16   E: **en las familias se ayudan y no más,**
            family members help each other that's all,
17   A: y qué
            so what

Emman repeatedly solicits help from Alicia in lines 3 and 11, but instead of collaborating with him, Alicia directs him to ask his partner in line 4 and flatly refuses his request in line 13. Meanwhile, Emman's partner, Junior, is toying with his lapel microphone, so Emman appeals to the group's organization by stating that "we are a family" in line 14. This leads to an increasingly sarcastic sparring match between Alicia and Emman over what helping is for a family. Ultimately, Alicia refuses to give Emman the answer and in so doing, she refuses to act like the "big sister," a role that Emman is trying to evoke from her. Here, Alicia, the lone girl in the group, distances herself from the girl's usual helping role and gets into a family-like argument over how families really collaborate, whereas Emman takes on a more sibling-like role as part of the general banter and rivalry between family members. Again, we see how the gender balance of the group influences the way in which these gender roles are enacted.

Interestingly, when the students really get involved in their work tasks and genuinely come together, they do not use any special labels such as "family" or "helping" to refer to what they are doing. Instead, they get swept up and fully engaged in the collaborative activity itself.

Gender Collaboration as Family Orchestrated Action

In example 9, the family group becomes so involved in their helping and collaborations on the task that they do not refer to their activity as helping. The task at hand is to find a meaningful sentence that defines the word "tongue." In their attempt to do this task, they engage in a joint search for a syntactic framework in which to place the answer, an orchestrated action in which each of the five members of the group offers candidate answers. In the course of this joint activity, Davina comments that a group at another table can overhear them and copy their answers. As she formulates the group work as a matter of "us" against "them," she acknowledges a competition between the families.

Example 9
Background: Kanani (K) is standing by the table at which George (G) and Amelia (A) are sitting across from Davina (D) and Jorge (J).

```
 1   J:   kay, wha' d' we ⌈ put  ⌉ here, ((shows paper))
 2   K:              ⌊ yeah ⌋
 3   A:   but we need another (.) thing (.) for over
 4        here.
 5   K:   ⌈ NO:, put ⌉ that, put ⌈ tha-     ⌉
 6   D:   ⌊ lookit   ⌋        ⌊ sh- th ⌋ ey can hea:r us,
 7        ((taps K's arm))
 8   J:   no:, ⌈ no:,       ⌉
 9   D:       ⌊ that's why ⌋ they're copying.
10        ((points to nearby table))
11   J:   no no no no no
12   K:   put it, PUT it PUT IT!
13   A:   the WHAT?
14   D:   we don't agree with you:.
15        (0.4) ((K erases))
16   D:   three against two.
17   J:   oh, somebody somebody ha-
18        doesn't have a tongue?
19        ((4 seconds of talk deleted))
20   J:   I got a
21   K:   I have a ⌈ tongue to lick.
22   J:            ⌊ tongue twister.
23   D:   tongue
24   K:   I HAVE A TONGUE (.) to lick.
25   G:   yeah yeah ⌈ yeah
26   D:            ⌊ to lick what:,?
27   K:   to lick sno ⌈ wballs,
28   G:              ⌈ slurpees slurpees slurpees⌉
29   A:              ⌊ THI::NGS, TO LICK        ⌋
30        ⌈ THI::NGS.
31   K:   ⌊ WE HAVE TO LICK SLURPEES
32   G:   yeah slurpees. yeah but we hafta- have to
33        think of what-
34        ((8 turns deleted))
35   K:   I have a tongue to talk with.
36   G:   yea:s..
```

37   K: ((to D & J))

38   I HAVE A TONGUE TO TALK WITH.

39   ((G, A, and K begin to write))

In example 9, the students become involved in a joint search for candidate answers to the question why we have tongues. Once they have the sentence frame "I have a tongue . . ." (line 21), members of the group suggest possible ways of completing the sentence as if they were in a verbal game. In the end, they all write down the shared answers at the same time. Here a girl, Kanani, takes the lead by ordering the others to write the sentence (lines 5 and 12). Despite this, both boys and girls collaborate on the sentence completion task as if this were a familial activity, where one person can add to another person's turn because they are all so familiar with each other's experiences and ways of talking. Although in this task the student group acts as a collaborative team, they do not invoke either the guiding metaphor of family or the idea of helping. The entire focus of their activity is collaborative and the task itself becomes the focus; girls to a large extent take the lead as the boys, although cooperating, engage in joking and comments.

Intersection of Gender and Culture: Conversational Strategies That Make Family Collaboration Happen

Although girls can oversee their group's collaboration and not bid to dominate the proceedings, they at times might attempt directly to organize their group's activity and even take over the responsibility for seeing that the task is completed. In this way, the cultural scenario of an organizing "big sister" intersects with the gender dynamic of the group.

Example 10, an extended transcript of example 6, shows how Amelia rounds her group up to collaborate on the correction of the answer to the question "Does Mervin give Molly advice?" Her talk and gesture are designed to catch everyone's attention and encourage the group to come together. At one point, Amelia makes a circling gesture to symbolize the group's inclusiveness and show that she is addressing the group as a collaborative work entity. By directing her talk at the whole group, Amelia indirectly reminds the others that they are expected to accomplish the written task collaboratively. However, when the group does not join

Amelia on the task, and Davina opposes her attempts to correct the group's erroneous answers, she tries another strategy: She codeswitches to Spanish to target her partner George's cooperation. Because Davina is an English-dominant speaker, she becomes excluded from the conversation. This strategy is successful, and George and Amelia partner up to correct the English answer through their interactions in Spanish.

Example 10
Background: Jorge (J) and Davina (D) are sitting across from George (G) and Amelia (A)

```
 1   J:    teacher ((calls to teacher))
 2   G:    ((leans toward Joel)) estoy en la tres,
                       I'm on the third one
 3         I'm ⌈helping       ⌉ these guys, ((points to D & J))
 4   A:        ⌊{R>}WHAT⌋
 5   G:    >que no saben nada,<
           cuz they don't know anything
 6   A:    the Molly's, NO WAI:T ((stands up))
 7   D:    ((looks at Student Aide (SA) behind her))
 8         I'm ⌈only⌉ even on the third one,
 9   G:        ⌊kay?⌋ ((to Joel))
10   A:    we're wrong in the fourth one too:,
11   G:    ~QUÉ:?
           what
12   D:    that's for YOU:, I copied off YOU:!
13   A:    ALL OF U:S! ((makes circle around table))
14   G:    what, yo no ((turns back to his group))
                   not me
15   A:    en la cuatro estaba MA:L,
           in the fourth one it was wrong,
16         porque (tú/te) crees que dijo la maestra
           because you know what the teacher said
17         'e aquí (..) que DOES es como una pregunta?
           that here (..) that DOES is like a question?
18   SA:   do the fourth one with everybody, then you
19         can come back to this, ((to J))
20   G:    SÍ:, pero ésta estaba allá, te acuerdas?
           yes but this was there, you remember?
```

```
21          ((points to A's paper, returns to his work))
22    A:    MERVIN ESTÁ-
            Mervin is-
23    J:    ((to SA)) (          ) ((J and D laugh))
24    A:    entonces (.) tiene que ser ((taps G's arm))
            then         it has to be
25          {R>} Mervi::n gives ┌Molly adVICE.{<R}┐
26    D:                        └I wanta (          )┘
27    G:    yeah, Mervin- ((quickly shows his paper to
28          A then he starts erasing it))
29    SA:   ((to D)) well then pay attention to your family,
30    G:    eh- eh-
31    D:    but lookit, ┌they don't┐ want to help (us-)
32    G:                └Davina:   ┘
33    A:    Davina, Davina gimme your book,
34          (.) ((D hands A her paper)) thank you.
35    D:    take all the- take all- gimme all the words,
36    A:    NO, I'm not gonna take you all of-
37          >the words,< ((A erases D's paper))
38    G:    {R>}Mervi:n (.) asks Molly {<R}
39          (.) qué:? no se entiende, (era)
            what? it doesn't make sense, (it was)
40    A:    {W>} MERVI:N {<W}
41          (1.0)
42    G:    gives Molly,
```

In example 10, Amelia uses a strategy often used by children, and sometimes by adults, to resolve the problem of multiple possible recipients: saying something out loud and loudly without explicitly designating next speaker (lines 4, 6, and 13). Amelia addresses the whole group with a raised voice even though the context of a small group makes ordinary out-loud talk available for any person to respond. In this way, she makes it clear that she is bidding to be the organizer of the group, apparently taking on the "big sister" role of getting all the other siblings to focus on getting the task accomplished. She finally succeeds later in the episode when she takes it on herself to coordinate correcting the answers for everyone in the group, even erasing their wrong answers. Throughout this episode, the two boys go along with Amelia's "big sister" organizational strategies without much protest. Although the boys do not vie for control, the other girl at the table, Davina, does make some verbal protest (line 12) before she finally accepts Amelia's help (lines 31, 34, and 35).

Example 10 reveals a flow of activity with several conversations simultaneously occurring. The conversational subgrouping is not just gender based, boys against girls. Instead, it is group alliances that form and dissolve with language code shift playing a significant part in the dynamic of the interaction. In this way, gender and cultural expectation intersect in such a way that neither one dominates the other. Codeswitching becomes another way of realizing the group alignments, as when George and Amelia switch to Spanish and then together puzzle over the answer (lines 14–25). Jorge talks to the student aide in English as does Davina later in the episode. George from the beginning uses Spanish as a peer-group code to talk to his friends at the next table in Spanish and finally to collaborate with Amelia. Amelia first interacts with Davina in English, and later her "call to order" to the group is given first in English using a loud voice and second in Spanish, where it achieves its effect of rallying for support and bringing George into the collaborative activity. The codeswitch into Spanish alone does not in itself mark the group's collaboration. It is the contrast or opposition between the two codes that serves as the relevant signaling device. Codeswitching therefore is an essential part of the *group's* linguistic resources, and it plays a significant role in their management of group dynamics (Gumperz, Cook-Gumperz, & Szymanski, 1999). The choice of code—that is the codeswitch—marks a peer activity rather than a strictly classroom one, and yet again the girls dominate the task activity using both codes and several strategies to gain control of the others' attention.

Arguing About Group Control: The Unrecognized Activity

Because collaboration, the intended outcome of group work, often proceeds against a backdrop of unfocused talk, the chatter and verbal banter of the group often shifts into focused talk that is specifically task related or involves disputes over control and ownership of work and space. As the girls in these groups are more likely than the boys to attempt to control the activities of others, they are more likely to get into disputes and arguments over the outcome of their control efforts. We have referred to these argument sequences as the unlegitimated activity in the classroom. "Helping" is legitimated by the teacher's authority, but arguments go

unrecognized unless they get out of hand. However, as Rizzo (1992) pointed out, conflict in small peer groups has an important role, often serving
to establish bonds and explore permissible limits of friendship. In any
argument, as Rizzo pointed out, there is a significant difference between
direct verbal aggression and just arguing or conflict talk. The following
examples show how arguing can be used strategically by students to test
the boundaries of their school friendships, most particularly between the
girls who are likely to vie for leadership of a group.

In example 11, Sonia assumes the organizational role of a leader in
the group that has been designated by her numbered role in the group.
Each member is assigned to take charge of monitoring the discussion of
the question that corresponds to his or her numbered role. Sonia selects
Yolanda to answer her assigned question, but when Davina insists on
responding, an argument ensues.

Example 11
Background: Davina (D) and Yolanda (Y) sit across from Sonia (S) and George (G)

```
 1   D:    go ((points to S))
 2   G:    {R>} how was a bronte ⌈saurus, {<R} whatever⌉
 3   D:                          ⌊number three          ⌋
 4   S:    {R>} where will some of the places the
 5         dinosaur found their food,{<R}
 6         ((D and Y both raise their hand))
 7   S:    Yo ⌈landa m- ((looks at D)) but, shut up,
 8   D:       ⌊in the- >in the tree<
 9   S:    Yolanda,
10   Y:    u:hm=
11   D:    =trees.
12   Y:    trees.
13   S:    ((to D)) shut up,
14   D:    u:h,
15   S:    shut up, I'm gonna kill you.
16         (0.2) one more peep on you. (1.0) one more.
17   G:    come O:N, ⌈Sonia,      ⌉
18   S:              ⌊Ms. Sut⌋cliffe
19         ((Teacher's Aide (TA) nears group))
20   TA:   yeah,
21   S:    this DA-VI-NA, (0.2) Davina's telling
22         all the answers.
```

```
23   D:    no, all I'm telling her is jungle.
24   TA:   the what?
25   S:    Davina's I- I- I- call Yolanda, she tells me
26         this (.) question, an' Davina's shouting
27         ⌜out. ⌝
28   D:    ⌞I told⌟ her
```

This is an example of a dispute between girls who are vying for control of
their work group. Sonia takes on the role of organizer when she asks
Yolanda to give the answer. When Davina calls out the answer before
Yolanda can in line 11, she subverts Sonia's effort at control. The dispute
goes on for a number of turns until Sonia escalates it with a typical
expression of sibling rivalry in lines 13 and 15, "Shut up, I'm gonna kill
you." George, acting as a bystander, tries to take a conciliatory role in the
family to bring peace between the warring factions in line 17. However,
Sonia continues the dispute by complaining to the teacher in lines 21 and
22, and 25 to 27.

A similar dispute occurs in example 12, where Amelia and Kanani are
criticizing Davina for incorrectly answering the question "What advice
does Molly's mom give her about this problem?" The entire group, con-
sisting of three girls and two boys, take turns alternately reading out loud
the source question and arguing about what needs to be written in the
answer. The girls take the lead in the argument, whereas the boys confine
themselves to making comments on their own activities.

Example 12
Background: George (G) and Amelia (A) are sitting opposite Davina (D), Kanani
(K), and Jorge (J)

```
1    J:    {R>}Molly's problems ⌜i:s that she:: {<R}              ⌝
2    D:                         ⌞{R>} does Molly's MO:M,⌟
3          does Molly's mom give her about
4          this ⌜problem, {<R}]
5    J:         ⌞doesn't, how do you spell doesn't,
6    A:    no ⌜DOES:⌝
7    K:       ⌞does, ⌟ ((to D)) you did it wrong heh
8          heh heh heh
9    A:    ((to D)) you didn't do RIGHT.
10   D:    I copied HE::R. ((points to K's paper))
11   K:    ((to A)) duh, it's supposed to be adVICE,
```

```
12          ┌that's┐ why I put an arrow there,
13    D:    └O:W┘ ((hurts hand))
14    G:    I U ((stops writing, looks up))
15    K:    ((to A)) she doesn't know what the arrows
16          mean,
17    A:    ((to D)) .hh the arrows means that (.)
18          ADVICE ┌GOES OVER HERE!┐
19    D:               └I KNO:W, jus- ge-  ┘
20          get off me,
21    A:    sheesh, {W>} DOE:S {<W}
22    D:    {R>} DOES Molly mom give her about this
23          problem {<R}
24    K:    {R>} DOES MOLLY'S MOM GIVE HER
25          ADVICE? {<R} ((looks at D))
26    D:    DU::::H ((stands up to say this in K's face))
```

The two girls, Amelia and Kanani, are treating Davina as a noncompetent member of the group by talking about her to each other, knowing that Davina must hear what they are saying but not addressing her directly in lines 15 and 16. This is a very direct strategy of conflict also used among Chinese girls, as described in Kyratzis and Guo (2001). In line 26, Davina responds by using a peer term of abuse, *DU::::H,* meaning "dumb idiot," said loudly in Kanani's face.

CONCLUSIONS: SEPARATE WORLDS IN CONTEXT

Through interaction analysis of group organization and activity, we can see that the girls emerge as "big sisters" to their metaphoric classroom families, and that in many ways they themselves take on the responsibilities of an "elder sister." In other words, they act as cultural brokers to their metaphoric classroom family groups in somewhat the same way as they might in their actual families. Neither the girls nor the boys were always cooperative; in fact, much of the interaction time was taken up with verbal sparring, forming alliances in which gender-separate groupings had their part. We can only speculate in terms of these data that outside of the classroom in the context of peer play the findings of Goodwin and Thorne on gender borderwork might well be the dominant communicative style for these children. However, within the classroom context, gender becomes part of a larger cultural dynamic. The teacher's use of the family metaphor for classroom cooperation establishes a particular, culturally informed set of communicative expectations. These expectations serve to override gender differences during classroom work. The students in this setting engaged in family discursive practices. Although the students did enter into disputes and arguments over control and leadership, they also were able to cooperate in ways that matched the teacher's idealization of family communication.

These data show these third-grade Latina girls to be engaging in rather different classroom and school-gendered activities than the mainstream literature has shown. The girls take on responsibility for helping others to accomplish the group's tasks. Although they can interact successfully with the rest of the classroom as peers, they define their commitments to their classroom families in ways that show greater concern with other girls' actions than with the boys' actions. Recall the practices of gender exclusivity more typical of intrafamilial sibling conflict in examples 11 and 12. As Vasquez et al.'s (1994) study shows, the girls come to act as agents responsible for organizing and translating the needs and requirements of family to and from the outside world, yet in this setting they also shift in and out of alignment with their own gender peers. In this way, their actions are more in agreement with Thorne's (1993) mainstream playground study, "Girls and Boys Together: But Mostly Apart." However, the cultural frame of the Latino family superimposes itself on the gender dynamic of separate worlds, giving the children access to other ways of arranging their communicative priorities. The SWH's claim is that the two genders through middle childhood grow up to constitute two noncommunicating separate groups that rely on different verbal strategies (Maltz & Borker, 1982). We found no strong support for the claim. This does not mean, however, that gender plays a lesser role but rather that whatever the differences, these are played out within a cultural context established at the juncture of home and classroom. The tensions between differing cultural conceptions of gender within family–home discourse, school, and peer groups will continue, these will only be resolved in adolescence by allegiance to either a home- or peer-dominant culture (Mendoza-Denton, 1995).

A relevant question emerges: In what way will these differences in gender within a Latino cultural frame continue to be part of the girls' and boys' experience in their later peer friendships? For now, whatever being bilingual and bicultural does mean, it clearly addresses a duality of experience that, as this study shows, is already part of the students' daily life and might either sharpen or disappear as they grow older. We have referred to the examples in this article containing Spanish and English use as codeswitching, but another language reality exists here. For the girls and boys, the choice is not between two language codes but between an ethnic identity that incorporates a notion of gendered options within a specific set of linguistic choices at the intersection of language and gender. Mendoza-Denton (1995), in studying girl gangs in a Northern California high school, found that Latina girls encounter a conflict between a "Mexican"-based identity and its language and gender assumptions; in other words, a Chicana identity with a differing collection of both language norms and assumptions of a gendered self. Many years ago, Labov (1972) suggested in his studies of urban boys' gangs in New York that part of accepting an identity within a peer group means adopting a collection of group ways of speaking and interacting, whereas those who do not accept these group practices find themselves marginal to the group. Eckert and McConnell-Ginet (1995) further explored how such communities of practice form in teenage years and described how they present very specific choices at the intersection of language, class, and gender. For third-grade children such as those in this study, the classroom provides a choice of ways of speaking. Although the home world might present boys and girls with very different options than those in the classroom and peer worlds, at least in the data from this classroom, the interactional subgroupings of boys versus girls have yet to be polarized.

The world outside of school, for preteenage girls, is still a home-centered one. It is a life that finds its experiences, pleasures, and demands within a community of extended family, family friends, and neighbors. As Coates (1995) detailed in a study of middle-class British teenage friends, in the transition from early teen years to later years, girls move away from an easy acceptance of their home-based self; their talk shifts from "being constitutive of friendship" to a more self-conscious accomplishment of their femininity, with "different kinds of feminine subjects, some in direct conflict with each other" (p. 417). Work on adult Latinas has shown how the choices of speaking practices involve conscious decisions to not only remain in touch with a Latina self, but also use this identity to establish and maintain successful work and community relations with others (Gonzales Velasquez, 1995), and thus be able to switch codes with alternating ways of speaking. Developmentally, the girls in this article have yet to make any of these choices, but by their school classroom talk they demonstrate their sensitivity to the options that lie ahead. This article has shown that the SWH is reshaped through cultural and language differences.

NOTE

1   The Spanish language translations are given in italics after the original talk, but in the case of partial Spanish–English switches, the English is not repeated. To handle the nature of talk in the language arts classroom, two special transcription conventions are used: {R>} {<R} indicates reading aloud activity, and {W>} {<W} indicates voiced writing activity.

REFERENCES

Coates, J. (1995). Discourse, gender and subjectivity: The talk of teenage girls. In L. Sutton (Ed.), *Cultural performances: The proceedings of the Third Women and Language Conference* (pp. 401–419). Berkeley: University of California.

Cook-Gumperz, J. (in press). Girls' oppositional stances and the interactional accomplishment of gender: Young children between nursery school and family life. In H. Kothoff & B. Baron (Eds.), *Gender interactions.* Amsterdam: Benjamins.

Dunn, J., & Plomin, R. (1990). *Separate lives: Why siblings are so different.* New York: Basic.

Eckert, P., & McConnell-Ginet, S. (1995). Constructing meaning, constructing selves: Snapshots of language, class and gender from Belten High. In K. Hall & M. Buchholz (Eds.), *Gender articulated: Language and the socially constructed self* (pp. 469–507). London: Routledge.

Gonzales Velasquez, M. (1995). Sometimes Spanish, sometimes English: Language use among rural New Mexican Chicanas. In K. Hall & M. Buchholz (Eds.), *Gender articulated: Language and the socially constructed self* (pp. 421–446). London: Routledge.

Goodwin, M. H. (1990). *He-said-she-said: Talk as social organization among Black children.* Bloomington: Indiana University Press.

Goodwin, M. H. (2001/this issue). Organizing participation in cross-sex jump rope: Situating gender differences within longitudinal studies of activities. *Research on Language and Social Interaction, 34,* 75–106.

Kyratzis, A., & Guo, J. (1996). Separate worlds for girls and boys? Views from U.S. and Chinese mixed-sex friendship groups. In D. Slobin, J. Gerhardt, A. Kyratzis, & J. Guo (Eds.), *Social interaction, social context, and language: Essays in honor of Susan Ervin-Tripp* (pp. 555–575). Hillsdale, NJ: Lawrence Erlbaum Associates, Inc.

Kyratzis, A., & Guo, J. (2001/this issue). Preschool girls' and boys' verbal conflict strategies in the U.S. and China: Cross-cultural and contextual considerations. *Research on Language and Social Interaction, 34,* 45–74.

Labov, W. (1972). *Language in the inner city: Studies in Black English vernacular.* Philadelphia: University of Pennsylvania Press.

Lloyd, B., & Duveen, G. (1992). *Gender identities and education: The impact of starting school.* New York: St. Martin's.

Maltz, D., & Borker, R. (1982). A cultural approach to male–female miscommunication. In J. J. Gumperz (Ed.), *Language and social identity* (pp. 195–216). Cambridge, England: Cambridge University Press.

Mendoza-Denton, N. (1995). Language attitudes and gang affiliation among California Latina girls. In L. Sutton (Ed.), *Cultural performances: The proceedings of the Third Women and Language Conference* (pp. 478–486). Berkeley: University of California.

Moll, L., Amanti, C., Neff, D., & Gonzales, N. (1992). Funds of knowledge for teaching: Using a qualitative approach to connect homes and classrooms. *Theory Into Practice, 31,* 132–141.

Ortner, S. (1997). *Making gender.* New York: Basic.

Rizzo, T. (1992). The role of conflict in children's friendship development. In W. Corsaro & P. Miller (Eds.), *Interpretive approaches to children's socialization* (pp. 93–111). San Fransisco: Jossey-Bass.

Streeck, J. (1986). Towards reciprocity: Politics, rank and gender in classroom interaction. In J. Cook-Gumperz, W. Corsaro, & J. Streeck (Eds.), *Children's worlds and children's language* (pp. 295–326). Berlin, Germany: de Gruyter.

Sulloway, F. (1996). *Born to rebel: Birth order, family dynamics and creative lives.* New York: Pantheon.

Swann, J. (1988). Talk control: An illustration from the classroom in analyzing male dominance in conversation. In J. Coates & D. Cameron (Eds.), *Women in their speech communities* (pp. 122–140). New York: Longman.

Szymanski, M. (1996). *Organizing bilingual talk in activity: Spanish/English speaking third graders in classroom work groups.* Unpublished doctoral dissertation, University of California, Santa Barbara.

Thorne, B. (1993). *Gender play: Girls and boys in school.* New Brunswick, NJ: Rutgers University Press.

Vasquez, O., Pease-Alvarez, L., & Shannon, S. (1994). *Pushing at the boundaries: Language and culture in a Mexicano community.* New York: Cambridge University Press.

Research on Language and Social Interaction, 34(1), 131–147
Copyright © 2001, Lawrence Erlbaum Associates, Inc.

The Place of Gender in Developmental Pragmatics: Cultural Factors

Susan Ervin-Tripp
Department of Psychology
University of California, Berkeley

This article offers a commentary on the studies by Kyratzis and Guo, Goodwin, Nakamura, and Cook-Gumperz and Szymanski comprising the special issue. The special issue is situated in the history of gender studies in developmental pragmatics. The inadequately recognized role of cultural factors is highlighted.

After Lakoff (1973), at the crest of the U.S. women's movement, stimulated a flood of studies on gender contrasts in speech, a list of differences became recurrent: compete–cooperate, command–suggest, assert–hedge, dominate–comply. Maltz and Borker's (1982) seminal paper speculated that gender differences in talk had their origins in childhood gender segregation.

Maltz and Borker's (1982) paper appeared, along with one by Tannen (1982) on marital miscommunication, in a volume of papers in which Gumperz and his students applied his theories of cross-talk. Gumperz argued that cross-cultural misunderstandings could arise from identifiable differences in discourse conventions, pragmatic systems, and the linguistic signals used to convey meaning and signal the frames in which talk was to be understood—the contextualization cues for interpretation. Maltz and

I am indebted to Jiansheng Guo for very thoughtful comments on drafts. Correspondence concerning this article should be sent to Susan Ervin-Tripp, Department of Psychology, University of California, Berkeley, CA 94720. E-mail: ervin-tr@cogsci.berkeley.edu

Borker proposed that separate male and female peer groups in childhood created the conditions for developing different cultural systems and associated conversational behavior, leading to misunderstandings.

The time was ripe for the study of children's gender socialization. Hymes (1962) called for studies of language socialization, and Mitchell-Kernan and Ervin-Tripp (1977) and Ochs and Schieffelin (1979; Schieffelin, 1979) laid a groundwork for studies of child language pragmatics. The Maltz and Borker (1982) theory was a stimulus, as both a research topic and a presupposition for popular books, because it seemed to provide a convenient explanation for the practical problem of adult misunderstandings.

However, there were some reasons for skepticism. Maltz and Borker (1982) oversimplified the evidence available even then. It was apparent early on that gender could test central themes in sociolinguistics, having as much complexity as other social categories, such as ethnicity. The sociolinguistic themes of language divergence, network, role ascription, and identity tactics provided possibilities for comparison in different sociocultural conditions of gender socialization. The shifts in a speaker's linguistic features with interlocutor, activity, interactional goals, and other aspects of situation all could be studied in relation to gender.

Gender presents a special situation in which frequency of interaction and identity can be in conflict. Speech similarity has long been known to be a sensitive index of social identification. Ervin-Tripp's (1968) summary reviewed evidence already known at that time that language similarity between speakers increases with frequency of social interaction under conditions of equality and solidarity or identification, as in what is now called a community of practice. What happens in families where sex is different between conjugal pairs or siblings but there may be a lot of contact? We need comparisons of the effects of family composition, family interaction, and network membership of children, based on the network principle in the work of Milroy (1980) and Eckert (1989). Even home schooling provides a natural experiment.

In discussing dimensions of social variation in speech, Labov (1966) distinguished indicators, markers, and stereotypes or ideological images of speech according to social categories—the traditional meaning of stereotype in the social sciences. Role playing, questionnaires, and even metalinguistic comments by playmates might evoke stereotypes. He contrasted stereotypes with indicators, or speech differences between socially or geographically separated speakers that are neither noticed nor manipulated except by linguists—in American regional variants, for instance, the contrast in the more and less raised and rounded vowel variants of "roof." His third category, markers, both indicated group differences and could be altered in different styles of a speaker. The stylistic variation he studied was from self-conscious reading style to spontaneous conversation. He called this difference monitoring and attributed the changes to social anxiety when vernaculars are in contact with prestige varieties. He had independent markers of monitoring, in channel cues such as speech rate, that he claimed differ in monitored and vernacular styles. Since that time, the term *monitoring* spread to *monitoring Black* in the sense of deliberate use of African American vernacular English features to signal identity. Femininity could be a form of monitoring or a performance.

Most such sociolinguistic studies of similarity, going back to dialectology, have used traditional linguistic indices like phonetic features. Maltz and Borker (1982) and Gumperz (1982) referred to a much wider range of levels of language, including interactional tactics. Not so much is known, in fact, about the transmission of these other linguistic and pragmatic features.

Stylistic research (e.g., Eckert & Rickford, 2001) on writing has extended into oral contrastive styles. Such contextual differences clearly implicate changes in syntax and other levels of language. Most obviously, changes in activity, whether required from the circumstances or chosen by the speakers, alter the goals and hence the actions, topics, and so on at all levels of language.

Role-playing research, like Andersen's (1990, 1996), has shown that from an early age children are able to simulate the speech of others, first in terms of phonetic and prosodic features, then lexicon, speech acts, and eventually even subtle features like discourse markers. Andersen's research shows that it is possible to identify which features speakers are capable of changing according to circumstance. However, the activity marked as role play is only one way speakers take different voices, whether in building a narrative, making a joke, or accomplishing some interactional goal by a stance shift. A changing voice can allude to a person or a social category recalled by the speech. Codeswitching is an extreme case.

Speech accommodation theory (Giles & Coupland, 1991) implies that changing group composition from separate to gender-mixed groups might alter speech. According to this theory, our speech becomes more like that of the addressees we like or want to impress, according to our abilities, and less like that of the addressees we do not like. In this case, girls playing with boys might change their activities and discourse to accommodate.

On the other hand, divergence might lead to greater contrast in certain types of play. Some situational contexts maximize gender marking. If something in the context or activity evokes a different gendered reference group, we can expect that individual speakers might "monitor male," or masculinize, speech or "monitor female," or feminize, speech. Whether these changes are to what Labov (1966) called stereotypes in the usual sense, or to markers, remains to be seen. Speech accommodation theory has not been applied to pragmatic and discourse features. This is a call to the examination of situational effects on styles within the individual's repertoire, as for example in some of the articles in Eckert and Rickford (2001). Both group composition and activity effects appear in the work reported in this issue.

RANGE OF PAPERS

The articles in this issue draw on data that are varied in age, from infancy and preschool (Nakamura; Kyratzis & Guo) to middle childhood (Goodwin; Cook-Gumperz & Szymanski). Social dynamics will change with social development; thus, comparisons across age present confounding problems. The focus of the collection is on cultural contrast among Chinese, Japanese, Mexican American children of recent immigration, middle-class White Americans, and a heterogeneous California school sample. The activities studied range from the child-controlled activity of playground jump rope (Goodwin) to adult-enabled but peer-controlled play in the presence of adults (Kyratzis & Guo; Nakamura) to classroom activities where tasks are assigned by adults (Cook-Gumperz & Szymanski). There is a problem in comparison with so much variation; similar types of activities and the same ages across cultural environments cannot be contrasted directly. What can be hoped, given that range, is the emergence of some hypotheses about the factors involved and a look to future comparisons to fill in the gaps. In short, this is the hypothesis-forming stage of the enterprise. However, this evidence already disconfirms some widely believed generalizations.

CROSS-CULTURAL VARIATION

According to the separate worlds hypothesis (SWH), biology is not destiny, but it is social grouping by gender that produces results that look like genetic bias, as if males and females create separate subgroup cultures. Gender cultures could be similar from one American sample to another if there is a macrocultural effect from family or school socialization by adults or older children, or from corporate culture through commercial influences. A more serious test is whether the separate worlds exist, and are alike, cross-culturally. Whiting and Edwards (1988), on the basis of an extensive program of careful observation in many widely diverse societies, concluded that "girls get more practice in nurturance and pro-social dominance, boys in egoistic dominance and challenge" (p. 278). However, this difference, they added, could be the result of gender socialization through adult assignment of girls and boys to different settings and tasks in the societies they studied. It could disappear if these activity contrasts did not exist. Kyratzis and Guo head straight for a cross-cultural critique of the SWH to which Kyratzis (1992) contributed supporting data earlier.

SETTING AND ACTIVITY CHOICES

Where adult society sets up a model of strongly contrasting concerns and settings for men and women, should we expect children to pick up on that contrast? However, this would only happen if gender is salient in the local family and school culture as a social dimension. There is no reason to presuppose that girls do not want to be Superman, or boys to play mother. Kyratzis (1994) found, indeed, girls who invented "Superkitty."

In Japan as in the United States, there were strong contrasts in the settings usually chosen by children in schools: rough-and-tumble play, trucks, cars, and superheroes versus playhouse and tea party for girls, but there was overlap in that both chose blocks and playing store. In the U.S. data, girls chose the dollhouse area more, boys the block area more, and Marx and Kyratzis (1998) found active resistance by preschool boys to domestic play as they got older.[1] Marx and Kyratzis confirmed, and Nakamura confirms, Thorne's (1993) observation of peer pressure regarding activities by the late 3s. Marx and Kyratzis reported that there was more pressure on boys than on girls in their sample.

INTERACTIVE EXPOSURE EFFECTS

One would expect that boys and girls on the margins of peer groups, children with twins or older siblings different in sex, or offspring of single parents, might show variation in language features related to gender. The whole interaction network of a child needs to be studied (Barker & Wright, 1951; Eckert, 1989). Boys and girls in families and neighborhoods do not live in isolation from each other, and play networks in neighborhoods can be fortuitous as well as chosen by young children. Girls might be in neighborhoods where there are no other girls and, as a result, might play with boys in boys' preferred activities. Several of these studies address factors that can reverse or neutralize the behavioral contrasts seen in the separate worlds research. The SWH assumes that the child's network is primarily of the same gender and also that the child's reference group is gendered.

Nakamura is the best placed to raise these questions, both because the Japanese language has such pervasive gender marking and because she followed children in both school and home and, thus, of the authors in this group, comes closest to observing their whole network. Because Japanese women usually stay at home with young children and fathers work late, mixed-sex nursery schools are, for both boys and girls, sometimes the most important contact with masculine speech outside of TV. Nakamura points out that this is especially true of firstborn children. Therefore, some girls' speech becomes more masculine when they enter preschool. At the school, children who preferred mixed-sex play groups had different language use patterns, so that, according to Nakamura, "a 3-year-old boy who preferred to play with girls sometimes the used feminine sentence-final particle *wa,* a 5-year-old girl who preferred to play with boys consistently used masculine linguistic forms" (p. 38). Of course, we do not know from the standpoint of identity marking which came first, friendship choice or linguistic features that may reflect speech accommodation.

ADDRESSEE AND ACTIVITY EFFECTS ON
LINGUISTIC FEATURES

The Japanese data provide a valuable extreme in the extent of linguistic contrast between expected male and female speech, affecting self-reference, lexical choices, addressee-governed politeness levels, and pragmatic tactics. Although these contrasts are discussed normatively in Japan, Nakamura and other recent work on adult Japanese speakers suggests that in practice there is considerable variation as well as historical change. These so-called gender contrasts are also setting- and addressee-related, not just speaker-determined, however, so that women at work sound more masculine and men talking to babies more feminine. Each child displays variation. Nakamura has shown that quite young children know self-reference forms, sentence-final particle probabilities, some lexical forms, and phonological styles that have feminizing or masculinizing effects.

How are these contrasts learned and maintained? Nakamura, who collected data both in homes and at school and with a peer, commented that peers were more likely to tease, taunt, and reject deviants, with pressure on both boys and girls. The U.S. data show examples of both boys and girls pressuring conformity from boys (Marx & Kyratzis, 1998). Is there less pressure on girls?

FRIENDSHIP GROUPS

Because peer groups are important sources of language pressure to conformity both in speech activities and speech styles, we can compare the composition of friendship groups. Thorne (1993) and Marx and Kyratzis (1998) looked at groups over time in schools and noted that as children mature, they join larger groups, and larger groups are more likely to be homogeneous in gender. Age-homogeneous groups were also more likely to be gender homogeneous. In families and neighborhoods, on the other hand, children play with the child at hand, and differences in age or gender matter less. Certainly, we can expect that neighborhood, school, and culturally specified activities all will affect these groupings and the knowledge they provide.

The differences Kyratzis and Guo found in preschool group composition may also be related to the type of play normal in groups of various sizes. Kyratzis found that mixed-sex larger groups did borderwork that we might expect would maximize speech divergence.[2] In the U.S. preschools she studied, she observed that in mixed groups of three or more, play occurred that downgraded female roles so that girls might have decided to play in girl-only groups instead. This cultural practice, which Kyratzis found but Guo did not see in Beijing, where teachers set up groups, can be consequential for group composition.

These issues definitely change with age, along with the type of play. In the middle childhood playgrounds Thorne (1993) and Goodwin studied, certain types of play were open and accessible to newcomers, and others were less so.

The composition of groups appears to affect speech in large measure through the choice of activities. Lampert and I, in an analysis of Garvey's data on the CHILDES database, studied changes in children's humor in preschool dyads that were selected as male pairs, female pairs, and recombined mixed pairs. We thus could see the same child with a different partner, as Guo could. There were strong gender differences in single-sex dyads. Boys engaged in more buffoonery and naughtiness, girls in verbal play and dress-up. The mixed groups were in between: Girls sang and did wordplay significantly more when paired with a girl than with a boy, but with boys they engaged in more physical clowning and less verbal humor (Lampert, 1996). It appears that children's activities are negotiated, and as Marx and Kyratzis (1998) reported, the same child can shift with different play partners to different kinds of play, with consequences for gendered speech features. Kyratzis and Guo report that in mixed preschool U.S. groups, boys were dominant, girls compliant. Girls asked questions, asked permission, and gave explanations more than boys did in such groups. However, mixed groups in China did not reveal the same contrasts at all; therefore, we cannot assume that these differences are universal. As Kyratzis and Guo note, the relative number of boys and girls in a group may alter activity preferences and dominance.

In looking at situational effects on gendered features, Nakamura notes that when playing with other girls, girls' speech had more beautification forms, hedges, collaborative sentence-final particles like *ne* and *no*, and speech acts such as asking questions and asking and giving permission. These feminine forms appeared primarily in role play, whereas the speech between girls out of role play was neutral. They must reflect the types of roles the girls were representing in their play.

With male peers, boys increased assertive speech and frequency of adversarial particles like *yo* and *zo*. Because they often played superheroes with other boys, it is not surprising that they had a high rate of making commands. In contrast, boys might play more feminine games with the mother when no peers were present, but we do not know how much their speech was adjusted to the context. These differences in form related to gender are more extreme cases of the types of speech act differences Kyratzis (1992) and Kyratzis and Ervin-Tripp (1999) found for same-sex best friend dyads in play settings.

CONFLICT

The "separate cultures" theory predicts that in mixed groups there should be evidence of culture clashes and misunderstandings. Speech accommodation theory predicts accommodation unless the children dislike each other or they are in a gender-marked activity. If we look at conflicts that occur in mixed groups, we see no such evidence of cross-gender misunderstandings.

Kyratzis and Guo (1996) found that conflicts in the U.S. preschool sample occurred mainly in terms of the planning of play. In the Chinese data in Beijing and Taipei, on the other hand, conflicts were part of role-play enactment or being funny (e.g., male–female teasing over "nuisance" behavior). There was no evidence that these conflicts arose from misunderstandings. In my data on Anglophones learning French from playmates in France (Ervin-Tripp, 1986), I found a theme in role play might be teacher and naughty pupil, allowing the teacher to display authority and punish the pupil. This naughtiness was programmed into the script by the children.

In the Chinese data, boys also play at "nuisance" with each other; therefore, it is not specifically reserved for mixed play.[3] Kyratzis and Guo interpret teasing by being naughty as a form of establishing intimacy. This is an argument compatible with recent research on teasing showing that when done in a friendly, not hostile, key and equitably distributed, teasing increases group cohesion (Keltner et al., 1998).

DOMINANCE

The Chinese naughtiness play provides an opportunity for girls to play roles of power in mixed groups. In the Chinese preschool data, boys were more compliant with girls' orders than with boys', and girls could undertake punitive roles in play, even to the extreme of a girl scolding her "father" (Kyratzis & Guo, 1996).

The Chinese data make it clear that in gender-mixed groups, hierarchy and domination are possible by girls, given dominant numbers or appropriate activities. In school-age children, Goodwin also found, first in her African American studies (Goodwin, 1990) and later in her work on jump rope, that girls in their own territory were competent in conflict and competition, and did not provide mitigations more than boys.

Cook-Gumperz and Szymanski show us another case where girls can be powerful. A school has defined cooperating mixed-gender groups of children as a "family." In these families, it was often the case that girls took the lead in organizing the group tasks. This frame, when invoked, licenses girls to be powerful. Female power is seen in girls' sarcastic, mocking statements and boys' compliance in these classrooms. It is not clear whether this leadership derives from the metaphor of the mother in the Latino family, who has power within the household, or from the power of the teacher. The techniques of control are similar to those used by teachers, namely raising the vocal volume or codeswitching to get attention or identify separate exchanges.

The girls Cook-Gumperz and Szymanski describe display a variety of tactics of domination and resistance. One girl subverts another's dominance, and another rebels and subverts the collaborative assessment of two others.

POWER AND TERRITORY

From the earliest ages of mobility, territory is identified with persons or groups (e.g., Daddycar, Mommycar). The first factor that appears to be important in defining who will be in power is territory. In my work on requests, I was surprised to find that territory affected mitigation. In requests between adults in an office requests from outside to inside an addressee's territory were mitigated (Ervin-Tripp, 1976). Kyratzis and Guo (1996) noted that girls and boys played together in the block area, but when they did so, boys were dominant. The block corner in that grade in that school was male territory.

Goodwin's study shows us a microhistory of social change. We see that at the beginning, jump rope was female territory. The consequence was domination by the girls. This domination was displayed in many ways—by commands from the girls and compliance by the boys, control of rules by the girls, and control of access. However, the development of expertise by the boys altered the power relations, giving boys less subordinate status in the activity. This change was only possible, of course, because of the school culture that did not promote territorial segregation.

In some societies, there is a power division by territory, with females in the family having power within the household and males having power outside the household. Representations that identify relative power only on the basis of outside roles may not represent gender accurately (e.g., Arab families, as in Morocco; Davis, 1980). Kyratzis and Guo explain the finding of female power in Chinese domestic scenarios by generalizing that women carry more power inside a household, to which males comply. Cook-Gumperz and Szymanski suggest similar power in Latino families.

Kyratzis's data are contrasted in that they show a dispreference for family play (Marx & Kyratzis, 1998) and a downgrading of female power in other mixed-sex activities such as doctor play (Kyratzis & Guo, 1996). Boys' dispreference for mixed-sex family play may eliminate possible occasions for girls to exert power. Home is apparently not a territory of power for mainstream U.S. females. The data here suggest that courtship might be the only context of mixed-sex play where American preschool girls could assert dominance, unlike their Chinese counterparts, who do appear to assert power in domestic arenas (Kyratzis & Guo, 1996). The pattern of request forms in middle-class U.S. families, as documented by Ervin-Tripp, O'Connor, and Rosenberg (1984), which suggests less power for mothers than for fathers and children, is also consistent with a devaluing of the home domain in American culture. The downgrading of women in U.S. families appears to be visible to youngsters 4 years old (Andersen, 1990), as seen in elicited family roles in puppet play.

EXPERTISE AND POWER

The question raised by Goodwin's results is the relation between territory and expertise. When boys and girls are assessed by the same criteria in mixed groups, traditional territorial dominance can give way. Does expertise trump territory? After 1 month of practice, as boys become more skilled, those who are most skilled issue directives and metastatements and receive questions. However, in the last game, girls still defined the important parameters of play.

"Boys begin to use the aggravated directive style of girls when they become more skilled in the game. The use of imperative forms and counter moves is related to acquired skill rather than one's gendered identity," according to Goodwin.

Kyratzis and Guo raise a similar issue about expertise in their analysis of shifting dominance in the studies of interaction over a Play-Doh "machine." In the Chinese data, male and female domination could be construed as based on domains of skill, with girls dominant in moral and emotional topics and boys in technical, gadget issues, even when the play materials were the same. Here changing the topic or activity can be a tactic for assuming dominance.

GENDER DIFFERENCES

Are speech contrasts simply a consequence of the typically different setting and activity selections by boys and girls? In some settings, no differences appear. A student in my lab, Elena Escalera, observing snacktime, found no gender contrasts at all in talk with a same-sex friend in an activity that is neutral.[4]

Yet, gender often remains a strong variable. In some studies, even when the same toys are presented, boys and girls, on average, did different things with the same toys. According to Nakamura, preschool boys more often fight and throw things; girls spend more time planning than enacting with the same play material. Girls do more family scripts, boys do more good-guy–bad-guy scripts of the sort seen on TV (Kyratzis, 1992). When Nakamura tried to establish comparable situations, she found that boys' dialogue was still dominated by challenges, conflict, and commands and contained slang and masculine terms. The girls' talk was comparatively neutral. Boys might use feminine language with the mother but would not do so with other boys, whereas girls used some masculine forms when in rough-and-tumble play and fighting. Kyratzis and Guo (1996) found that even when Guo tried to control setting and materials with Play-Doh in China, the boys and girls focused on different issues, which then affected their dominance in the interaction.

We do not know how robust these gender differences are. Marx and Kyratzis (1998) found only a few children were consistently masculine or feminine in speech style; the other children accommodated to partners and changed speech with activity setting. Even so, on average there were differences.

AGE CHANGES

The subtlety of tactics noted in the studies of children in middle childhood reminds us of the importance of pragmatic development, which has not been mentioned in these studies. We know that children age 7 or older can be aware of the perspectives of others and control a wider variety of speech acts and speech events. The complexity of their discourse is greater because they are more able to plan joint events and anticipate the responses and arguments of the other. There are examples of such skills in my work on requests (Ervin-Tripp, 1982). In Cook-Gumperz and Szymanski's examples, we see a 9-year-old able to anticipate and thwart power moves and retaliate against public criticism in a complex way. Dramatic examples have been given by Goodwin (1990), such as the imbedding of narrative into argument, thus shifting the participation framework and removing ground from the antagonist by publicly making him the butt of the narrative. This skillful complexity could be strategically forward looking, rather than just a series of ad hoc tactical maneuvers.

MECHANISMS OF PEER CONTROL

The SWH, as Thorne (1993) pointed out, assumes either a shared norm or uniformity of behavior, which is belied by the evidence. The strongest data on this point are the individual cases pursued longitudinal-

ly by Marx and Kyratzis (1998), who were able to show that certain children in the school they studied were bellwethers in displaying extremes of
gendered activity and speech, for reasons they did not explore. Other children who joined them in play, and in activities that are differentially gendered, momentarily increased the frequency of gender indexing in speech,
but another partner and another activity context could be neutral. The
boundaries available in public, especially in school, change through time
as norms develop and deviants are criticized. Edelsky's (1977) judgment
data suggest continued increase in stereotyping in middle childhood.

MONITORING AND CONSTRUCTING,
MARKING AND INDEXING

New constructs are being used in the discussion of speech variation—
for example, in a special issue of *Language in Society* (Holmes, 1999) on
gender in adults. How can we know whether speakers are "monitoring
feminine" or "indexing femininity"? Nobody has proposed an independent criterion; thus, we are left with descriptive categories that appear to be
interpretive. We can ask the same questions when we look at the discursive construction of femininity. Sex is physical, and already known to
friends, so it cannot simply be constituted by language except in role play.
However, femininity and masculinity can be. Is it happening only when
girls' behavior fits a stereotype and not at other times? Is it happening all
of the time when boys play together, and, if so,' what is added by this
description? These definitional and empirical issues need to be resolved
to keep the sociolinguistic study of gender from becoming simply a fash-
ionable change in the language of description. Then, we can clarify theoretical positions that can allow empirical disconfirmation.

Role playing is a valuable way to find out about children's knowledge
of sociolinguistic indexes when nothing is at stake. Andersen (1996) and
her collaborators had strong evidence that children come to recognize a
social feature, comparative power, that they can mark by choice of discourse markers. When children are displaying feminine or masculine
indexes, they may simply be identifying a role (e.g., mother, nurse, superhero or fireman); we cannot tell without finer grained controlled role or
judgment studies whether gender is indexed in the choice. And it could be

argued that the separation between role playing and real life is not absolute in either children or adults.

SUMMARY

These articles give a much more nuanced view of the variability across culture, age, and setting of gender marking and indexing in speech. They show us individual differences that may reflect either dispositional factors or network and socialization history. They show us that group size and composition, activity contexts, and expertise in the activity affect speech styles so much that linguistic features cannot be attributed to gender factors alone unless these contextual aspects are controlled. Above all, they provide questions about the cross-cultural generality of the Maltz and Borker (1982) speculations.

NOTES

1   Elena Escalera, who has observed half-time in a nursery school in Berkeley for 4 years, audiotaping for 2 years, noticed that boys did choose the playhouse domestic context when they were young 3s, but other boys pushed these boys to other forms of play as they got older.

2   *Borderwork* is a term used by Thorne (1993) to identify activities that rely on a clear male–female boundary, such as team games divided by gender, chasing, or kissing.

3   Escalera observed girls arguing over playing "bad girl" (personal communication, February 3, 2000).

4   Escalera's dissertation is in progress.

REFERENCES

Andersen, E. S. (1990). *Speaking with style: The sociolinguistic skills of children*. London: Routledge.

Andersen, E. S. (1996). A cross-cultural study of children's register knowledge. In D. I. Slobin, J. Gerhardt, A. Kyratzis, & J. Guo (Eds.), *Social interaction, social context, and language* (pp. 125–142). Mahwah, NJ: Lawrence Erlbaum Associates, Inc.

Barker, R. G., & Wright, H. F. (1951). *One boy's day; A specimen record of behavior.* New York: Harper.

Davis, S. S. (1980). The determinants of social position among rural Moroccan women. In J. Smith (Ed.), *Women in contemporary Muslim societies* (pp. 87–99). Lewisburg, PA: Bucknell University Press.

Eckert, P. (1989). *Jocks and burnouts: Social categories and identity in the high school.* New York: Teachers College Press.

Eckert, P., & Rickford, J. (2001). *Style and sociolinguistic variation.* New York: Cambridge University Press.

Edelsky, C. (1977). Acquisition of an aspect of communicative competence; Learning what it means to talk like a lady. In C. Mitchell-Kernan & S. Ervin-Tripp (Eds.), *Child discourse* (pp. 225–244). New York: Academic.

Ervin-Tripp, S. M. (1968). Sociolinguistics. In L. Berkowitz (Ed.), *Advances in experimental social psychology* (Vol. 4, pp. 91–165). New York: Academic.

Ervin-Tripp, S. M. (1976). Is Sybil there? The structure of some American English directives. *Language in Society, 5,* 25–66.

Ervin-Tripp, S. M. (1982). Ask and it shall be given you: Children's requests. In H. Byrnes (Ed.), *Georgetown Roundtable on Languages and Linguistics* (pp. 235–245). Washington, DC: Georgetown University.

Ervin-Tripp, S. M. (1986). Activity structure as scaffolding for children's second language learning. In W. Corsaro, J. Cook-Gumperz, & J. Streeck (Eds.), *Children's language and children's worlds* (pp. 327–358). Berlin, Germany: de Gruyter.

Ervin-Tripp, S. M., O'Connor, M. C., & Rosenberg, J. (1984). Language and power in the family. In M. A. K. Schulz & C. Kramerae (Eds.), *Language and power* (pp. 116–135). Belmont, CA: Sage.

Giles, H., & Coupland, N. (1991). Language: Contexts and consequences. Pacific Grove, CA: Brooks/Cole.

Goodwin, M. H. (1990). *He-said-she-said: Talk as social organization among Black children.* Bloomington: Indiana University Press.

Gumperz, J. J. (1982). *Interethnic communication.* New York: Cambridge University Press.

Holmes, J. (Ed.). (1999). Communities of practice in language and gender research [Special issue]. *Language in Society, 28*(2).

Hymes, D. (1962). The ethnography of speaking. In T. Gladwin & W. Sturtevant (Eds.), *Anthropology and human behavior* (pp. 15–53). Washington DC: Anthropological Society of Washington.

Keltner, D., Young, R. C., Heerey, E. A., Oemig, C., & Monarch, N. D. (1998). Teasing in hierarchical and intimate relations. *Journal of Personality and Social Psychology, 75,* 1231–1247.

Kyratzis, A. (1992). Gender differences in the use of persuasive justifications in children's pretend play. In K. Hall, E. Bucholtz, & B. Moonwomon (Eds.), *Locating power: Proceedings of the Second Berkeley Women and Language Conference* (Vol. 2, pp. 326–337). Berkeley, CA: Berkeley Women and Language Group.

Kyratzis, A. (1994). Tactical uses of narrative in nursery school same-sex groups. In M. Bucholtz, A. C. Liang, L. A. Sutton, & C. Hines (Eds.), *Cultural performances: Proceedings of the Third Berkeley Women and Language Conference* (pp. 389–398). Berkeley, CA: Berkeley Women and Language Group.

Kyratzis, A., & Ervin-Tripp, S. (1999). The development of discourse markers in peer interaction. *Journal of Pragmatics, 31,* 1321–1338.

Kyratzis, A., & Guo, J. (1996). "Separate worlds" for girls and boys?: Views from U.S. and Chinese mixed-sex friendship groups. In D. I. Slobin, J. Gerhardt, A. Kyratzis, & J. Guo (Eds.), *Social interaction, social context, and language* (pp. 555–575). Hillsdale, NJ: Lawrence Erlbaum Associates, Inc.

Labov, W. (1966). *The social stratification of English in New York City.* Washington, DC: Center for Applied Linguistics.

Lakoff, R. (1973). Language and women's place. *Language in Society, 2,* 45–80.

Lampert, M. D. (1996). Studying gender differences in the conversational humor of adults and children. In D. Slobin, J. Gerhardt, A. Kyratzis, & J. Guo (Eds.), *Social interaction, social context, and language* (pp. 579–596). Mahwah, NJ: Lawrence Erlbaum Associates, Inc.

Maltz, D. N., & Borker, R. A. (1982). A cultural approach to male–female miscommunication. In J. J. Gumperz (Ed.), *Language and social identity* (pp. 195–216). New York: Cambridge University Press.

Marx, T., & Kyratzis, A. (1998). Gender and contextual specificity: Play theme, make-up of the group, time, and status as influences on preschoolers' language and gender display in classroom friendship group interaction. In S. Wertheim, A. C. Bailey, & M. Corston-Oliver (Eds.), *Proceedings of the Fifth Berkeley Women and Language Conference* (pp. 333–346). Berkeley, CA: Berkeley Women and Language Group.

Milroy, L. (1980). *Language and social networks.* Oxford, England: Blackwell.

Mitchell-Kernan, C., & Ervin-Tripp, S. (Eds.). (1977). *Child discourse.* New York: Academic.

Ochs, E., & Schieffelin, B. (1979). *Studies in developmental pragmatics.* New York: Academic.

Schieffelin, B. B. (1979). *How Kaluli children learn what to say, what to do, and how to feel: An ethnographic study of the development of communicative competence.* New York: Columbia University.

Tannen, D. (1982). Ethnic style in male–female conversation. In J. A. Gumperz (Ed.), *Language and social identity* (pp. 217–231). New York: Cambridge University Press.

Thorne, B. (1993). *Gender play: Girls and boys in school.* New Brunswick, NJ: Rutgers University Press.

Whiting, B. B., & Edwards, C. P. (1988). *Children of different worlds.* Cambridge, MA: Harvard University Press.

Research on Language and Social Interaction, 34(1), 149

Acknowledgment

The following persons reviewed manuscripts in 1999/2000. Their support for the journal is deeply appreciated.

Charles Antaki, *Loughborough University*
Nancy Baym, *University of Kansas*
Shoshana Blum-Kulka, *Hebrew University*
Lisa Coutu, *University of Washington*
Anna DeFina, *Georgetown University*
Derek Edwards, *Loughborough University*
Angela Garcia, *University of Cincinnati*
Beth Haslett, *University of Delaware*
Scott Jacobs, *University of Arizona*
Timothy Koschmann, *Southern Illinois University*
Michele Koven, *University of Illinois*
Erina L. MacGeorge, *George Washington University*
Carol Myers-Scotton, *University of South Carolina*
Mark Rapley, *Murdoch University*
Jeffrey D. Robinson, *Pennsylvania State University*
Shirley A. Staske, *Eastern Illinois University*
James Taylor, *University of Montreal*
Robin Wooffitt, *University of Surrey*

For Product Safety Concerns and Information please contact our EU representative GPSR@taylorandfrancis.com Taylor & Francis Verlag GmbH, Kaufingerstraße 24, 80331 München, Germany

Batch number: 08153776

Printed by Printforce, the Netherlands